A Year of
Zero Waste Sewing

A Year of Zero Waste Sewing was originally written and published as a series of zines during 2022-2023.

Cooatalaa Press
PO Box 1014
Clare 5453
Australia

ISBN: 978-0-646-89137-8

Technical editor: Anthea Martin
Editor: Nan Berrett, Word Solutions
Cover by Stu Nankivell, Blue Goanna Digital

This book was written on Ngadjuri land and Liz Haywood pays her respects to Elders past and present.

www.lizhaywood.com.au
@lizhaywood3754
Resources and video links to accompany this book
can be found at: lizhaywood.com.au/resources-for-ayozws-book/

NATIONAL LIBRARY OF AUSTRALIA

A catalogue record for this book is available from the National Library of Australia

A Year of
Zero Waste Sewing

*A year of exploration, making and musings on
zero waste patterns and clothes*

Elizabeth M Haywood

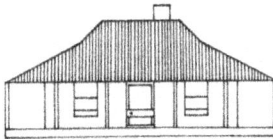

COOATALAA PRESS

Contents

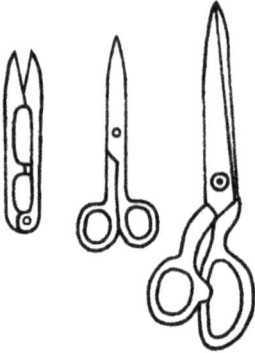

Concepts

People

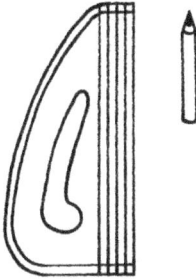

Projects

Questions

A brief

Introduction

Welcome to *A Year of Zero Waste Sewing*, a book jam-packed with ideas for making zero waste sewing patterns and reducing textile waste.

There are multiple ways of doing zero waste - this book is mainly concerned with design, but there are lots of other approaches too, such as repurposing scraps, using discarded or post-consumer textiles, re-fashioning, mending, and so on. These are all very legitimate and needed as we confront the problem of waste in the fashion industry and our wardrobes.

Zero waste comes under the umbrella of creative patternmaking, and is an uncommon yet very exciting way to design. It's *so* different to how we normally design clothes, and can be described as "backwards designing"; the design typically emerges from the pattern and cutting layout, instead of the other way around, and brings about fresh design details and silhouettes. There's no correct way to make zero waste patterns - it's a creative and experimental design process.

The material in this book was originally published in monthly instalments as zines, over the course of two years. During the process of writing I made zero waste home sewing patterns, gave talks, did consulting and discussed issues with other makers, all of which helped gel new ideas swimming in my head. From this, I firmly believe that both *making/doing* (lots!) and *collaborating* brings about the greatest riches of actionable concepts, and I encourage you to experiment with cutting techniques, connect with other patternmakers and importantly, show your work.

I've had lots of fun with zero waste. I hope you do too! Cheers! Liz x

January

Compostable Closures
...and fastenings from found objects

One of the considerations of sustainable clothing is its end-of-life. Even with diligent mending and the very best clothes care, all clothes will eventually reach the point where they are worn out. What will happen to it when it can no longer be worn? Will it be thrown in the rubbish? Or recycled (either at home or a recycling facility)? Is it compostable?

A complication with recycling and composting is the garment's haberdashery. That is, the things other than fabric used to make it, such as labels, sewing thread, fastenings and embellishments. These are typically made of a different material and either won't compost at all or can't be separated easily for recycling.

A garment's fastenings are always an important design consideration and more so for sustainable clothing. Almost all of the ones we generally use aren't compostable, but have been in use for so long we don't even think about them.

Zips, alas, aren't compostable. Even if the tape is made of cotton, the teeth, which are made of metal or plastic, won't decompose.

Wait a minute - doesn't metal rust away? While metal doesn't rot or decompose like fabric, yes, eventually it will disappear over a *long* time. Because of this, metal fastenings such as **press studs**, **hooks**, **rivets**, **jeans buttons**, **eyelets** and **buckles** generally aren't considered suitable for a backyard compost bin.

Nylon and polyester are types of plastic and won't decompose—fastenings include **Velcro**, **no-sew snaps**, **nylon press studs** and **plastic buttons**. **Polymer clay buttons** contain plastic. Glass and porcelain buttons won't decompose.

For home sewn clothes, some of these things can be unpicked and reused on something else.

If you're designing for compostability, there are still plenty of things you *can* use. Often it's these limitations that bring out the best in our creativity and stretch us, in the same way zero waste pattern cutting does.

Historic fashion books might give you some inspiration.

You can design the closure to be **integral with the garment's design**, for example wrap-arounds, 3-armhole garments, lacing, belts, ties, or tabs and flaps. Often these use the same fabric as the garment.

3 armholes

Or none: the garment could pull on over the head (in stretch or non-stretch fabric), be open fronted or have an edge-to-edge front.

Fun fact: George Lucas's costume design brief for *Star Wars* stipulated no zips or buttons; apparently they didn't have them in a galaxy far, far away. Take a look at the costume designers' solutions next time you watch it.

How about elastic? Natural rubber will compost, but currently it's hard to get elastic without synthetic covering over the rubber.

There are button materials which *do* decompose, for example wood, casein (milk), corozo (tagua seeds), coconut shell, horn, shell, bone, bamboo and rubber. They won't rot at the same rate as the rest of the garment but eventually they will break down.

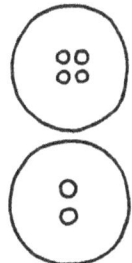

Some compostable buttons you can make

Watch a video of these: https://www.youtube.com/watch?v=TpuNJLGGAK8

Thread buttons were used for men's shirts circa late 17th—early 18th century. They were also called Dorset birdseyes. The button is made entirely from heavy linen thread, thicker than sewing thread. If you don't have any handy, try perle cotton or sashiko thread. If you're recycling, the heavy thread from the top of flour bags or feed sacks is suitable. A button takes about 1 metre/yard of thread.

1. Wind the thread about 30 times around a stick. A 5mm knitting needle will make a button about 1cm/⅜" wide; the end of a pencil will make a slightly wider button. **2.** Remove the thread from the stick and thread a needle with the end. Optional: stitch through the centre and around the circle of thread several times to hold it. **3.** Work buttonhole stitches around the circle. **4.** On the back, stitch across several stitches and work buttonhole stitches over them to make a shank. **5.** Finished button back. **6.** Finished button front. It may or may not have a hole in the centre.

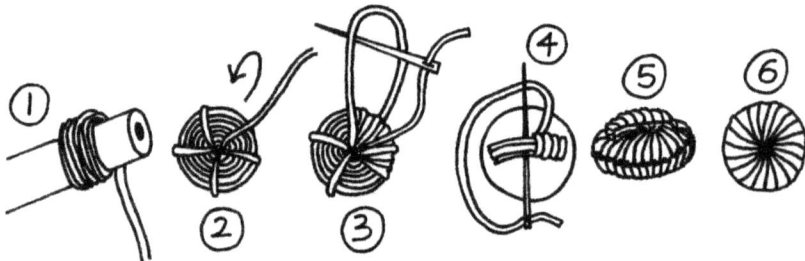

A firmer button has a **core of fabric** rather than thread. **1.** Take a 5cm/2" square of fabric and cut it in half diagonally. You only need one triangle. **2.** Roll it up finely, starting at the long edge. It helps to moisten your fingers. **3.** Wind the fabric tube around the end of the stick and proceed from Step 2, above.

✂ Choose a fabric the same colour as your thread.

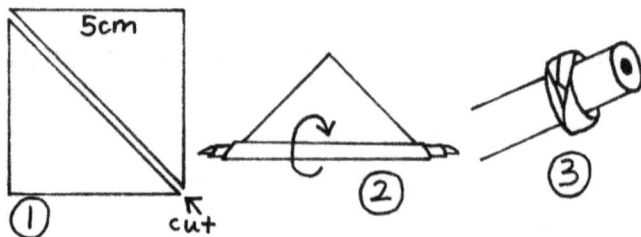

4

Medieval self-stuffed buttons are spherical.   They're made using fabric and very strong thread.   **1.** Cut a square of fabric about 5cm/2". Trace a circle on it and work running stitches on the circle.   **2.** Pull up the thread, stuffing the corners inside.   **3.** Work another circle of running stitches around the edge as shown and pull it very tight.   **4.** The finished button.

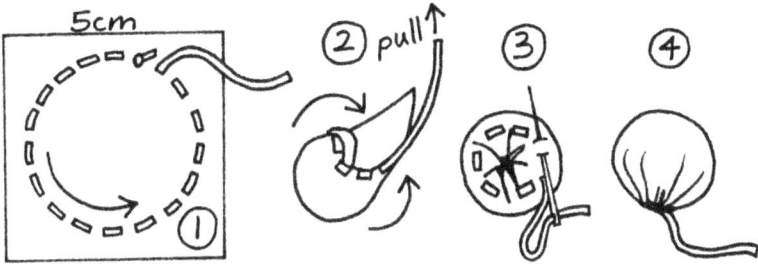

Ball buttons, typically seen on Chinese qipao, are made from fabric rouleau or cord. They fasten with a loop which is often ornamental. **1.** Begin with a loop. **2.** Loop the cord over the first loop. If you're using rouleau, keep the seam facing down. **3.** Loop the cord again, weaving through the first two loops. **4.** Ease the loops into a tight ball shape.

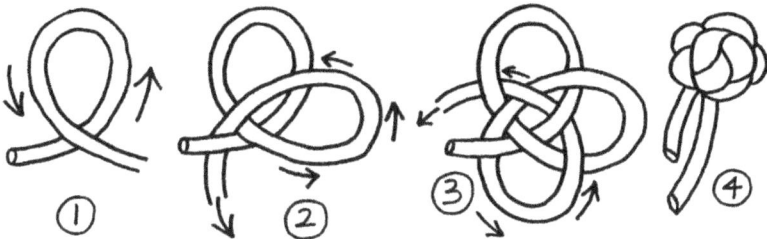

Leather toggle buttons are also called chap knots.   Is leather compostable?   It's skin, so yes, but there's some question whether the tanning chemicals will affect the soil.   You could also use boiled wool or rubber. **1.** Cut a triangle with a fine point. Halfway along, punch two holes. **2.** Roll up the triangle and weave the point through the holes. **3.** Pull tight.

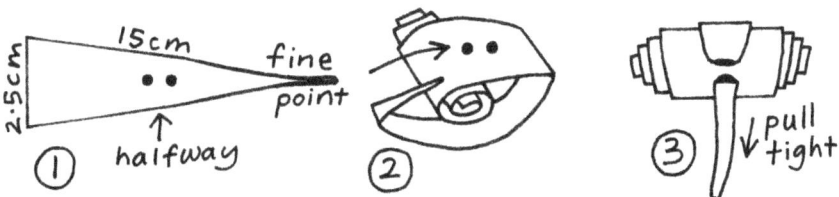

Some other buttons to investigate...

Dorset buttons are made with thread worked over a metal ring.

Singleton buttons are a type of Dorset buttons made with fabric rather than thread. Dior used them on his white New Look jacket in 1947.

Macclesfield buttons are made by wrapping thread over a wooden button mould.

Fastenings from found objects or rubbish

Can you make buttons or other closures from found objects? Or things in the recycling bin or that are being thrown away?

For example, placemats, rubber boots, rubber thongs, hot water bottles, old belts of any type, old camping gear, fan belts, bicycle inner tubes, lego bricks, computer hardware, basketballs or other broken sports equipment.

✂ If a shape is unsuitable to slip through a buttonhole, or if it would damage a buttonhole, use a loop to close it.

✂ If the button can't be washed in the same way as the garment, make it removable like a **cuff link.** →

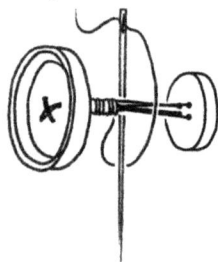

Used **beer bottle tops**. Hammer the washed bottle tops flat, hammering the crimped edge inwards. Make the holes with a nail. For larger buttons hammer the crimped edge outwards, but be aware the rough edge may damage the fabric. Helmut Lang featured these in his SS 2004 collection.

Make **wooden button**s from a fallen tree branch or prunings. Cut the branch into 3mm thick rounds using a hacksaw. Drill 2 or 4 holes using a fine drill bit. Sand the button smooth. Finish the buttons using oil and beeswax. You could also make toggles.

Buttons from pebbles. Choose tiny smooth rounded pebbles. Drill holes using a Dremel with a diamond tip, submerging the pebble in water while you drill.

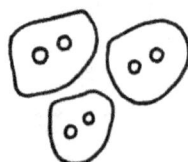

Designing a Pocket Matrix

A **pocket matrix** is a modular shape containing all the pocket pieces nested together.

One approach to zero waste pattern cutting is to make modular pattern pieces, where all the pieces are squares and rectangles and can be moved around the fabric. It doesn't mean curves can't be incorporated, as long as the outside perimeters of each module are straight.

Pockets of any type are often cut from small areas in the cutting layout, around the big pieces, but they can also be designed as stand-alone, moveable modular pieces. This works well if you're going to cut the pockets in a different fabric.

The first pocket matrix I designed looked great on paper but didn't work in reality. It was for exterior pockets on a pinafore/overalls pattern I was making. Unfortunately, after much trying, I couldn't get the proportions right so I abandoned it.

It looked like this: The pieces separated to make these:

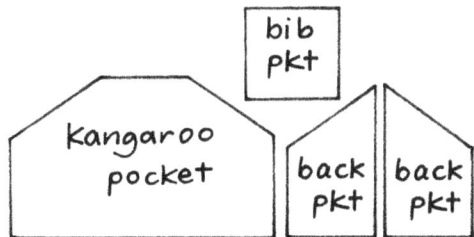

bib
pkt

Kangaroo
pocket

back
pkt

back
pkt

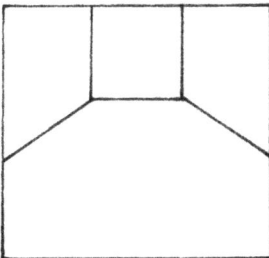

Another unworkable
version was this:

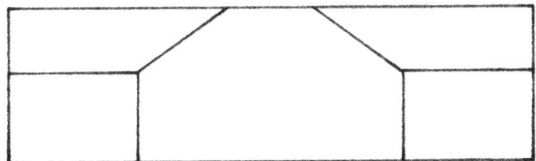

7

However, I really liked the idea, and eventually made **in-seam pockets** that looked like this:

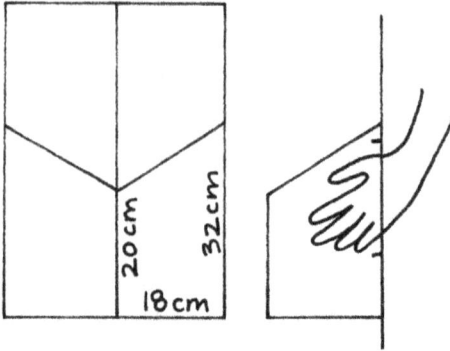

Note that this shape on its own won't give you a pair of pocket bags - it needs to be mirrored.
You need to commit to two pockets!

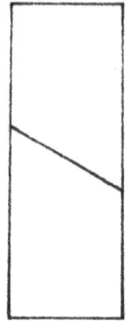

20cm 32cm 18cm

I've since used this pocket idea for other patterns too:

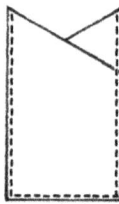

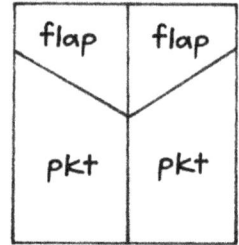

lapped patch pockets   zippered   pockets with flaps

flap   flap

pkt   pkt

Here's another example, for a **cutaway patch pocket** with a little coin pocket. The whole piece could be cut twice (as a pair) to make a strong, self-lined pocket. Or, it could be cut as a single layer pocket with the curved openıng bound or faced with bias binding.

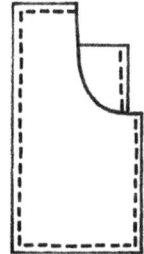

Alternatively, the pieces could be cut like this....

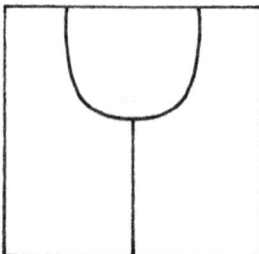

...to make a pocket like this:

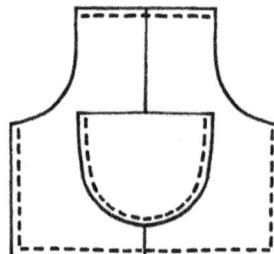

Of course, many pockets are square shaped anyway. The pocket bags for the welt/jet/flap pocket family are all rectangles and therefore easy to cut zero waste. If you want rounded corners to avoid pocket lint, cut them square but stitch them curved.

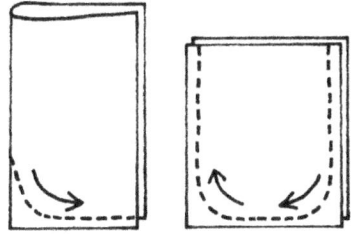

If you're making a zero waste pattern for a garment that will be cut in multiples, rather than singly, consider a **tessellating pocket shape**. A tessellating shape will perfectly interlock with itself.
At each end you'll have half-shapes - what to do with these? You may decide to make some pockets with a seam through the middle.

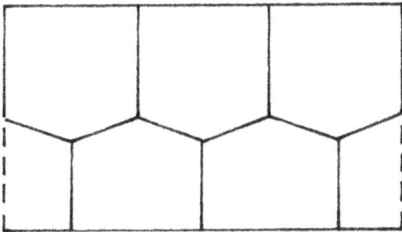

A jeans back pocket shape.

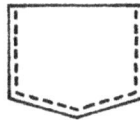

A chiselled edge patch pocket and pen pocket.

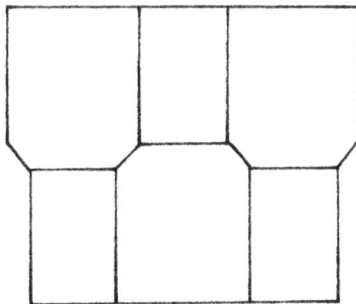

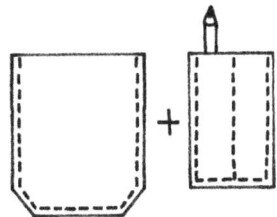

A gusset can be added to any patch pocket to give it a new shape.
and...
Graph paper is excellent for designing tessellating pocket shapes.

ZWdc

Zero Waste Design Collective (ZWDC) is dedicated to providing online alternative educational resources on zero waste design and building an international community of designers, teachers, industry stakeholders, home sewers, students and enthusiasts.

"The seeds of ZWDC were sown through Cassandra Belanger's challenging experience studying a Masters in Fashion + Textiles in Glasgow. She was interested in studying zero waste fashion design but there weren't any teachers that could help her. She had previously worked on a zero waste design project with Holly McQuillan and decided to ask if Holly would be available to share her expertise. At the time, Holly was working on her PhD at the Swedish School of Textiles in Sweden. So Cassandra applied for funding and managed to organise a trip for Holly to visit Scotland and teach a week of zero waste fashion design workshops to Cassandra and her fellow students. During this time, in 2018, Cassandra and Holly became friends and spent the week geeking out over zero waste fashion. When the week was over Cassandra realised the issue around lack of access to education and resources about zero waste fashion design. Holly expressed the desire to stop travelling for workshops as she had been concerned about the environmental impact and the time away from her family. Cassandra pitched the idea to Holly to develop some online classes and resources to respond to the needs mentioned. Leading up to 2020, and when the pandemic hit, their ideas were put into focus.

Accessing quality education in zero waste design was a recognizable gap in the fashion education system. Many people wanted to learn about zero waste design but didn't know where to start or how to find resources. Our initial vision was to produce accessible, quality education to those who desired to learn more about zero waste fashion design. Early on we realised we needed to expand the team to ensure a range of skills and to increase capacity. We asked the two best zero waste designers we knew of to join us - Danielle Elsener and Mylène L'Orgilloux. Together we formed the international Zero Waste Design Collective, and began to formulate a clearer vision for the future of zero waste design education.

Over time we recognised that as well as resources and education, there was a need for a community around zero waste design in order to bring our vision to fruition. We believe a partnership of community and education is vital to the success of creating a waste-free fashion industry. We all need support and encouragement on our journey to a better fashion future and we desire to fill that need through our global online community. We help people connect through our online Community Directory. We are so excited to see the global zero waste fashion design community flourish and grow as people find one another and connect on their journeys."

Danielle Elsener is a zero waste system designer who works to dispel industry problems through design, education, and manufacturing. She is the founder of DECODE MFG in Brooklyn NY, the world's first ZW manufacturing facility. @decodecodecode

Cassandra Belanger is a maker, designer and community educator with an emphasis on zero waste and sustainable making practices. Originally from Canada, she lives in Glasgow, Scotland. @stitcherystudio

Holly McQuillan is a researcher, designer and educator in her role as an Assistant Professor in Multimorphic Textile Systems at TU Delft, Netherlands. @holly_mcquillan

www.zwdcollective.org   @zwdcollective
Contact us at: zwdcollective@gmail.com

Ask Lizzy

Q: Is the grainline important with zero waste patterns?

A: Yes, absolutely, the grainline is always important with any pattern, including zero waste. The grainline affects how the fabric hangs when it's worn, because the grainline is aligned with the threads in the cloth.

It can be tempting to rotate a pattern 5%-7% off grain to fit it in the layout better, *but don't do it!* Sure, sure, in some circles it's considered totally legit, but start messing with the grainline and there's no telling where you'll end up. Some say disrespecting the grainline is a downhill slide to ruination and could ultimately end your patternmaking career.

There are many mistakes in sewing which can be fixed, but a garment that's cut off-grain can never be corrected. The garment will twist around the body, seams won't hang straight and you risk people crossing to the other side of the street rather than walk past you wearing it.

Q: Is it harder to do alterations on zero waste patterns?

A: Yes. With zero waste patterns, the cutting layout IS the pattern. If you change one piece, the pieces around it will be affected. Because of this, it's hard to merge sizes - for example, if you wanted to cut a size 14 dress with size 16 hips.

But there are ways that designers can help with this. Bigger seam allowances, if only at the side seams, can allow clothes to be altered. (hypocritically, I write this with almost all my patterns having measly 1cm seams, but I vow to change from now on). Ditto deep hem allowances.

If the zero waste pattern is for home sewing, guidance on choosing a size and fitting advice is always welcome, because size inclusivity is not just about size/measurements, it's about shape as well. Anticipating fitting needs for *various shaped* bodies embraces more users.

February

Putting Curves in
Zero Waste Patterns

Using Selvedges

Zero Waste Stories: Thread Faction

Ask Lizzy

Putting Curves
in zero waste patterns

I won't lie: curves can be hard to put into zero waste patterns.
Geometric shapes such as squares, rectangles, trapezoids and even triangles are easier to use, because the fabric itself is straight not curved. While geometric shapes can give some beautiful silhouttes, putting curves into zero waste patterns is highly satisfying and can result in some delightfully unexpected fashion designs.

One way that I incorporate curves is to use an existing, regular, pattern and take a close look at the convex and concave shapes to see if I can nest them together. If they don't fit neatly, the shapes might be able to be tweaked to make them fit. I decide what *really* needs to be curved and if it would be OK to cut it straight or semi-curved instead. Sometimes straight pieces can be made curved using darts. The important thing is not to try and re-create the original, but to keep an open mind for a fresh, new design.
When starting off, it's easier to work on something that's a single size such as a bag, toy, quilt etc, or a one size garment.

Here's another way I've used – a real-life example, where I put a curved shape into a square one and built a pattern around it. The key with this method is to put the curved shape/s into the layout *first*.

1. This curved shape is a Peter Pan collar, taken from a dress pattern. It already has seam allowances on it.

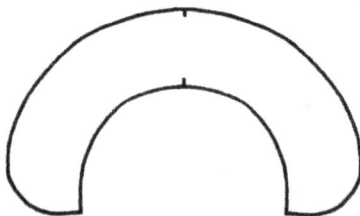

14

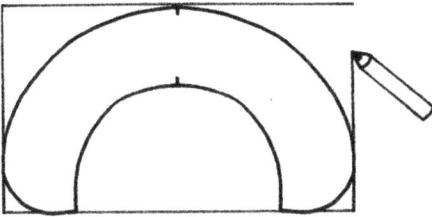

2. If we draw a rectangle around it, it gives us the collar with four difficult-to-use triangle-y shapes and a potentially useful semi circle.

3. However, if we extend the rectangle so it's not directly around the collar, some useful shapes start to appear.

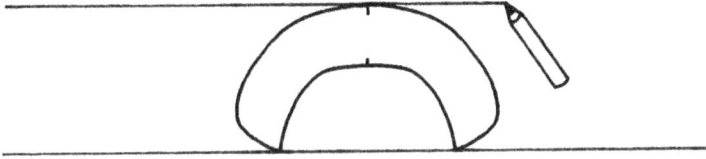

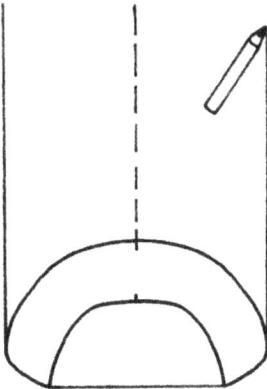

The rectangle could alternatively be extended in the opposite direction.

4. Maybe the large shape could be a front or front facing? Its neckline could be the shared edge with the collar. Or, it could be a strip running on top of the shoulder, from the neck to the wrist, like a strapped shoulder.
Or it could be part of a cutaway pocket depending on how long it's cut - the length of this piece hasn't been determined yet.

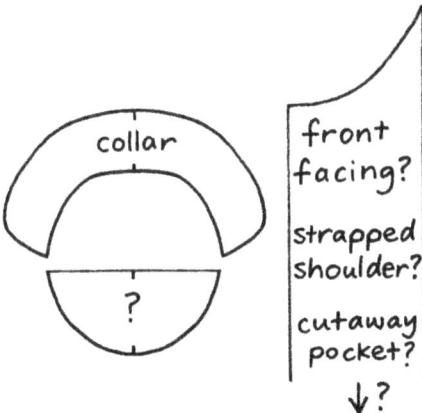

collar

?

front facing?

strapped shoulder?

cutaway pocket?

↓?

15

5. What about the semi circle? It doesn't have to stay a semi circle - it could be cut up to make several shapes, or extended to make a bigger pattern piece. It could even be used as part of a different garment which is cut with this one.

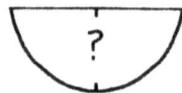

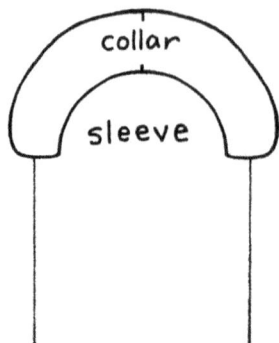

6. However, we have to be careful with interlocking shapes if we're making multiple sizes. If we used the semi circle for a sleeve head, for example, we would run into trouble with bigger sizes, because a collar won't grow as much as the sleeve head - the collar will stop growing after about a 107cm/42" bust, but the sleeve will keep on growing. Therefore the semi circle would be best used for something like a pocket, frill or facing which won't need to grow much.

7. At some point, I would frame it with a rectangle/square that's the fabric width, to help work out the rest of the pieces.

You can start to see from this exercise that creating a zero waste pattern can be a vastly different process from traditional flat patternmaking where a block is adapted to interpret a designer's sketch.
With zero waste, the design reveals itself *as the pattern is being made*, rather than a pattern being made from a sketch.

Here are some other thoughts.....
✂ Don't be afraid to adjust shared edges to change the shapes - it could give a more interesting collar shape and better neckline. In other words, it doesn't *have* to remain a Peter Pan collar.

✂ Being non-precious with shapes will open up more possibilites - the more rigid you are with what *can't* change, the less choices you have and the harder it is to make a pattern.

16

✂ Curved shapes contained within square modular ones can give very flexible zero waste layouts, because the pieces can be moved around to fit different width fabrics. If there are any offcuts, they'll all be highly useable rectangular ones.

✂ When starting to make patterns in this way, aim for *just one* curved shape (collar, sleeve, yoke, etc) and build the rest of the pattern around it.

✂ Keep it simple. Take the advice an old senior cutter gave me when I was a junior: *The simplest layouts are often the best. If possible, mark out half the fabric then mirror it.*

Here's what the layout eventually looked like.
It became a short sleeved blouse with a rounded collar, back yoke and front buttons.

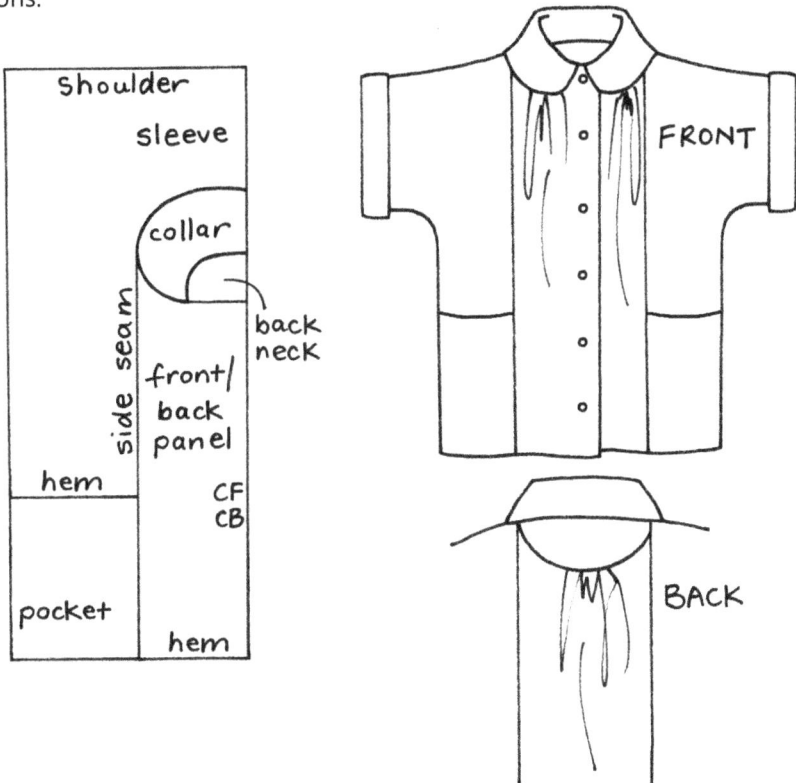

Using Selvedges

Zero waste proponents are pretty hot on using the selvedges, preferably in an artistic way. Certainly, if one is to claim 100% fabric usage, the selvedge should be used in some way.

My entire training and career has been decidedly *anti*-selvedge.

I worked for 9 years as a factory clothing cutter and I've seen a lotta selvedges. The most beautiful selvedges (typically on expensive fabrics) were flat, smooth and barely visible. The worst ones were wide, uneven, hairy, with big needle holes punched in them and they were woven tighter than the fabric - we had to snip them to get them to lay flat.

In factories, selvedges are trimmed off and either thrown away or (more often) hung from a hook for anyone to use. The most common use for them is to tie up bundles of cut work for machinists, but there's a host of other useful factory applications: tying power cords out of the way, hanging up cardboard patterns, winding around scissor handles to make them more comfortable (fleecy is best for this), holding open the broken roller door until the repair man comes, tying back hair when you forgot a pony tail elastic, etc etc. Anything but use them in clothes!

Fun fact: *Selvedge* is the British English spelling, and *Selvage* is the American English. The terms selvedge and selvage are a corruption of "self-edge". The type of loom used will affect the selvedge's thickness, appearance, density, width and weave.

It's been a conscious effort to use the selvedges rather than throw them away. Selvedges can be used in clothes either secretly, where only the wearer will see them, or openly, on display as an embellishment.

Here are some handy ideas for using selvedges....

✂ The obvious use for selvedges is as a **seam finish**. It makes for faster sewing, as you don't have to neaten the edge, and it preserves the integrity and strength of the cloth since it isn't cut.
It's sometimes seen on the centre back seam of vintage skirts and dresses.

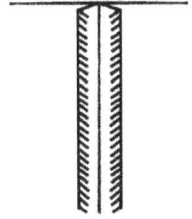

✂ Some selvedges, especially on wools, have **useful information** woven in, such as Pure New Wool, or Made in England etc. These are nice to keep intact somewhere inside the garment.

MADE IN AUSTRALIA (I WISH!)

Also, if the fabric is designed by a particular artist, it honours them to keep the selvedge with their name on it in the garment.

✂ **As a stabiliser instead of cotton tape.**
Trim off a 6mm/¼" or narrower strip of selvedge to use. It can be the same or a different fabric. The selvedge of silk organza is excellent to use - if you're cutting silk organza for any purpose, save the selvedges to use for this. Also, selvedges which are woven too tightly to use for anything else can be cut off and used as stabiliser.

Places that might need stabilising are: faced waistlines, faced necklines, pocket edges, shoulder seams that might stretch, V-necks and wrap dress necklines.

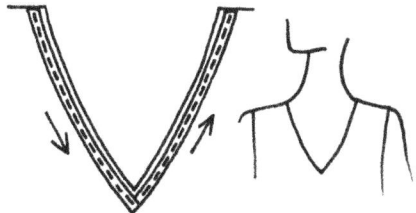

19

✂ Insert the cut-off selvedge into a seam or edge, as **a kind of piping**.
It could be a good look on denim or other fabrics with interesting selvedges.

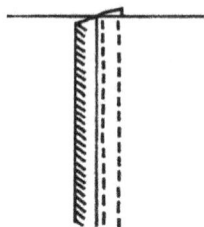

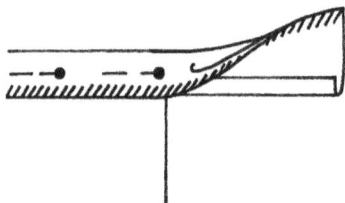

✂ Use the selvedge **on one side of binding**.
You could put it on the inside or outside, and it will give a flatter finish than turning under the edge.

✂ **Self-finish a facing.**
For example, the edge of a facing on an unlined (or lined) jacket. Of course, it only works for facings with a straight edge.

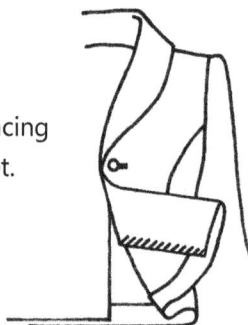

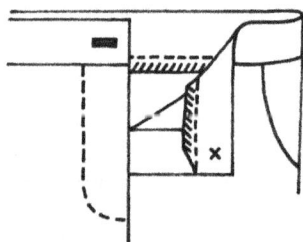

✂ For the **inner edge of a waistband**.
Use the selvedge instead of overlocking, binding the edge or folding it under.

✂ **Beltloops.**
Use the selvedge for one edge of a beltloop to reduce bulk. It could be used underneath or on top.

✂ Follow Chanel's example and make use of the selvedge as a **trim**.

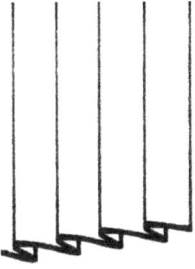

✂ Use as a hem.

A selvedge is the least-bulky hem you can make! Use the selvedge on the edge of kilts or other pleated pieces.

✂ The edge of a ruffle or rosette.

These can be made from a long strip at the edge of the fabric.

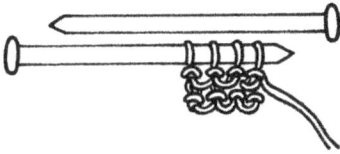

✂ Use cut-off selvedges like **yarn.**
The strip can be knitted, crocheted or macramé'd to make perfectly colour-matched trim or embellishments.

What if the selvedge is totally unsuitable to use?

Sometimes the selvedge shrinks when you wash a piece of fabric, making it unsuitable to use as-is. However, the selvedge could still be used if you cut it off - maybe you could use it as stabiliser tape.

Other times, the selvedge is too rough-looking or too damaged to use.

Maybe you can find a household use, such as....

....tying up plants in the garden....keeping items bundled in your linen cupboard....emergency shoelaces....tying back the kitchen curtains....fixing the broken string on the Totem Tennis....keeping printed-out book manuscripts together....bundling up things together before slipping them into a post satchel....tying up fabric offcuts to keep them together in your stash....anywhere you can tie things together instead of using a bag.

thread faction
s t u d i o

Zero Waste Stories

Liz Elliot of Thread Faction Studio designs zero waste patterns for everyday childrens' clothes.

Thread Faction Studio is a small independent sewing pattern company in Queensland, Australia. Specialising in everyday childrenswear for their Zero Waste PDF pattern range, Thread Faction supplies a resource for home sewers around the world to start on their zero waste sewing adventure, and is dedicated to contributing to the greater conversation in and around zero waste design.

Liz Elliott has the most traditional of sewing backgrounds. Taught to sew by her mother and grandmother at age 6, she sewed first for her soft toys, then for herself as she grew, sewing from patterns, then making alterations, then designing from scratch. Liz arrived at her middle thirties, at home with the kiddos, with close to 30 years of home sewing and patternmaking experience under her belt. Thread Faction Studio began.

"Through the course of running a sewing pattern design business, the amount of fabric waste involved in sewing mainstream garment patterns quickly became evident. Drowning in fabric scraps, I became enchanted with the idea of zero waste design. The concept presented an elegant solution to the problem of using up scraps: just do not make any.

I researched the zero waste movement with great enthusiasm,

22

devouring all the reading material that I could find, from Timo Rissanen & Holly Mcquillan's book on the concept, to Julian Roberts' Subtraction Cutting, to the work of independent pattern designers and amazing fashion design students.

From that research, and subsequent zero waste pattern making explorations, it quickly became apparent that designing for zero waste was not an exact science.

When beginning with zero waste, patterns were often simplified to a slightly different shape. These shapes are reminiscent of traditional or folk clothing, which is frequently based on squares and triangles to allow the pieces to be slotted together more easily without any fabric scraps remaining. This does result in wearable garments that indeed produce no waste fabric, but the squared-off garment often uses more fabric than cutting a similar garment in the conventional way. So, from a modern home sewing perspective, where garments are not often disassembled and the fabric reused, the sewer has had to purchase more fabric and the garment may not fit quite as well as the original design – there did not seem to be any point in this design direction.

Wanting to avoid this outcome, and to ensure that Thread Faction Designs are not just a gimmick but designs that the home sewer will genuinely use, I approach zero waste design for children's sizing following these guidelines:

1. All pattern pieces for a particular garment need to fit, without waste, into a rectangular shape. So, although this still creates 'waste' when compared to the width of the fabric, all offcuts are very usable rectangular pieces.

2. Be mindful that the zero-waste version of the garment created does not use more fabric than making the same or similar garment using the conventional pattern making method.

3. Keep the creativity in check regarding 'using up' extra pieces of fabric and not adding embellishments only to 'use up' the extra fabric.

4. Be mindful of choosing styles just because they are easier to create using the zero waste method.

5. Lastly, stay true to the Thread Faction Studio regular pattern making mantra: make the types of designs that children wear every day."

www.threadfaction.com   @lizatthreadfaction

Ask Lizzy

Q: Is it really OK to turn pattern pieces around and cut them across the fabric? Isn't the warp direction stronger?

A: Yes and no. Or rather, it depends. It's OK for most things. We already cut some garments around the other way, for example to position a border print. A great advantage with zero waste patterns is that it gives you the space to make the garments wider; garments grow in width more than length as the sizes increase (see page 129).

But you need to be careful with it! The warp direction is more prone to shrinkage than the weft, so you need to be absolutely certain the fabric won't shrink (because instead of the garment getting shorter with shrinkage, it will get narrower). You generally can't cut knit fabrics in the other direction, because you need the greatest stretch to go around the body. Clearly it won't work for napped fabrics and directional prints.

Yes, the warp direction *is* stronger, and the weft direction tends to be a little bit stretchier. If you're making jeans for example, which need to be strong and have some give around the body, then cut them the regular way.

So, really the answer is: it's OK most of the time but decide according to your specific fabric and garment.

Q: Do you need training in regular patternmaking first before attempting zero waste patternmaking?

A: This is a question I've chewed over for some time. (I'm a formally trained conventional patternmaker.) I think regular and zero waste patternmaker training can easily exist side-by-side, and I even think no training is necessary provided a person has experience with sewing, altering patterns and an enquiring mind.

March

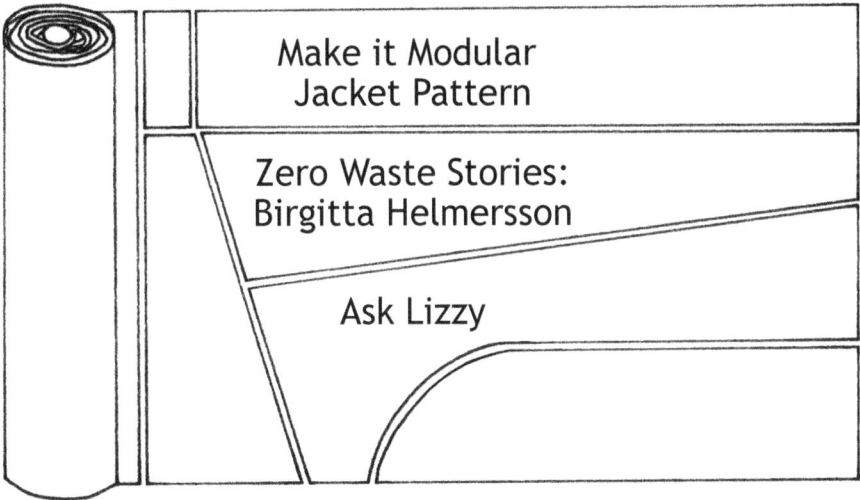

Make it Modular
Jacket Pattern

Zero Waste Stories:
Birgitta Helmersson

Ask Lizzy

Make it Modular
Jacket Pattern

I'm a big fan of square/rectangular modular pattern pieces. They can be easily moved around the fabric to fit any fabric width, and any offcuts are easy-to-use-later rectangles. Modular doesn't mean the pieces can't have curves (although this jacket doesn't have any), as long as the curves are contained within the straight sides.

This is a very simply shaped jacket and the pattern is like a basic recipe - you can follow it exactly and make a very wearable jacket, or you can "cut your cote after your cloth" and adjust it to fit the fabric you have.

For example, you can make it any length you like, change the collar (to be narrower, shorter, longer or absent), tweak the width of the front panel, adjust the armhole depth, or change the belt or pocket.

Simple shapes like this lend themselves to bold fabrics or embellishments.

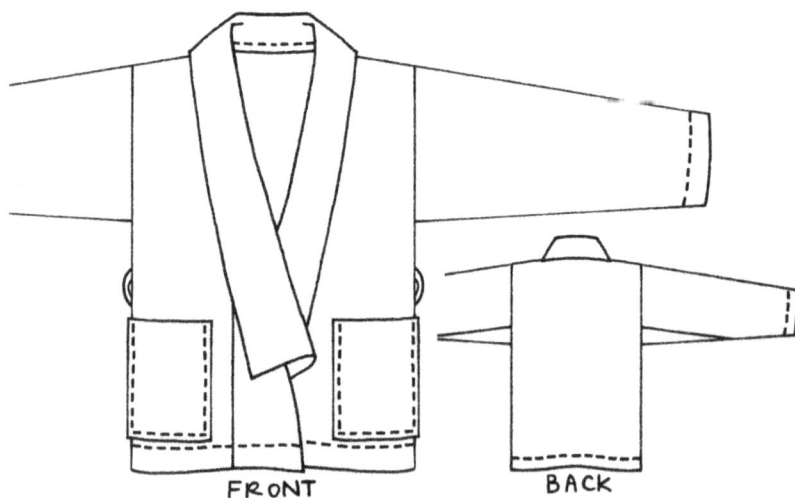

FRONT   BACK

Choose a size. There are 20 sizes, to fit approximately a 32" bust to a 70". Pick a size according to the *finished size* jacket you want - measure one you already have and compare it to the chart. I recommend having at least 25cm/10" wearing ease. To measure a jacket, lay it flat, do it up, then measure from side to side and double it to find the finished body circumference. Measure the "wingspan" across the jacket from wrist to wrist.

Size	A	B	C	D	E	F	G	H	I	J
Finished body circumference	106.6cm 42"	111.7cm 44"	116.8cm 46"	121.9cm 48"	127cm 50"	132cm 52"	137.1cm 54"	142.2cm 56"	147.3cm 58"	152.4cm 60"
Finished wingspan	150.4cm 59¼"	153cm 60¼"	155.5cm 61¼"	158.1cm 62¼"	160.6cm 63¼"	163.1cm 64¼"	165.7cm 65¼"	165.7cm 65¼"	165.7cm 65¼"	165.7cm 65¼"

(Chart continued)

Size	K	L	M	N	O	P	Q	R	S	T
Finished body circumference	157.4cm 62"	162.5cm 64"	167.6cm 66"	172.7cm 68"	177.8cm 70"	182.8cm 72"	187.9cm 74"	193cm 76"	198.1cm 78"	203.2cm 80"
Finished wingspan	165.7cm 65¼"	165.7cm 65¼"	165.7cm 65¼"	165.7cm 65¼"	165.7cm 65¼"	165.7cm 65¼"	165.7cm 65¼"	165.7cm 65¼"	165.7cm 65¼"	165.7cm 65¼"

Suitable fabrics include plains, stripes, wovens, boiled wool, stretch wovens, knits, napped fabrics and directional prints. Checks are fine to use but might take a little more fabric to match the checks. The collar can be cut in a different fabric - maybe you have a special piece of fabric you can use for it.
There are no fabric estimates. Either cut your jacket to fit the piece of fabric you have or lay the pattern pieces out on an imaginary fabric width and take a measurement.

Pattern pieces

1. The **front and back** pieces are rectangles. The **length** is your desired length + 5.5cm/2⅛" (for a 4cm/1½" hem and 1.5cm/⅝" shoulder seam).

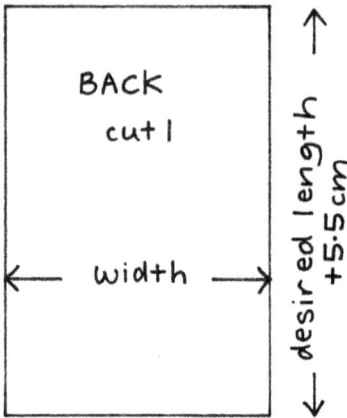

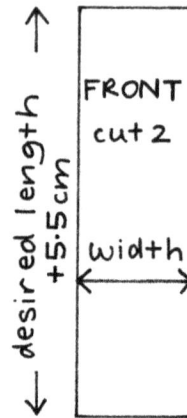

The **back width** is cut at:

Sizes A-B-C: 56.5cm/22¼" - 59cm/23¼" - 61.5cm/24¼"

Sizes D-E-F: 64.1cm/25¼" - 66.6cm/26¼" - 69.2cm/27¼"

Sizes G-H-I: 71.7cm/28¼" - 74.2cm/29¼" - 76.8cm/30¼"

Sizes J-K-L: 79.3cm/31¼" - 81.9cm/32¼" - 84.4cm/33¼"

Sizes M-N-O: 86.9cm/34¼" - 89.5cm/35¼" - 92cm/36¼"

Sizes P-Q-R: 94.6cm/37¼" - 97.1cm/38¼" - 99.6cm/39¼"

Sizes S-T: 102.2cm/40¼" - 104.7cm/41¼"

The **front width** is cut at:

Sizes A-B-C: 23.4cm/9¼" - 24.4cm/9⅝" - 25.4cm/10"

Sizes D-E-F: 26.3cm/10⅜" - 27.3cm/10¾" - 28.2cm/11⅛"

Sizes G-H-I: 29.5cm/11⅝" - 30.7cm/12⅛" - 32cm/12⅝"

Sizes J-K-L: 33.3cm/13⅛" - 34.6cm/13⅝" - 35.8cm/14⅛"

Sizes M-N-O: 37.1cm/14⅝" - 38.4cm/15⅛" - 39.6cm/15⅝"

Sizes P-Q-R: 40.9cm/16⅛" - 42.2cm/16⅝" - 43.4cm/17⅛"

Sizes S-T: 44.7cm/17⅝" - 46cm/18⅛"

2. The **front panel** forms the V-neck which is the lap-over part of the jacket.
Make the *length* the same as the *front cut length*+ 6cm/2⅜".

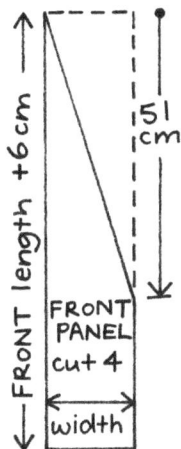

The **width** is cut at:
Sizes A-B-C-D-E-F+: 11.4cm/4½"- 11.7cm/4⅝" - 12cm/4¾" - 12.3cm/ 4⅞" - 12.7cm/5" - 13cm/5⅛"
However, the width can be up to 5cm/2" wider than this.
Measure down 51cm/20" on one side and draw a diagonal line as shown in the diagram.

You need to **cut 4** of this piece, as *two pairs* like this:

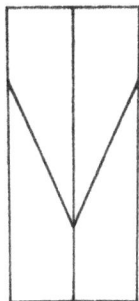

When you cut these, try and arrange a selvedge on the long side of one pair AND interface this pair. These will be the innermost front panels.

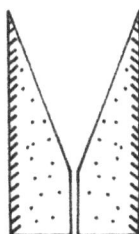

(diagram labels: FRONT length +6cm; 51 cm; FRONT PANEL cut 4; width)

3. The **sleeves** are rectangular. The **width** is cut at:
Sizes A-B-C: 45cm/17¾" - 46cm/18⅛" - 46.9cm/18½"

Sizes D-E-F: 47.9cm/18⅞" - 48.8cm/19¼" - 49.8cm/19⅝"

Sizes G-H-I: 50.8cm/20" - 51.4cm/20¼" - 52cm/20½"

Sizes J-K-L: 52.7cm/20¾" - 53.3cm/21" - 53.9cm/21¼"

Sizes M-N-O: 54.6cm/21½" - 55.2cm/21¾" - 55.8cm/22"

Sizes P-Q-R: 56.5cm/22¼" - 57.1cm/22½" - 57.7cm/22¾"

Sizes S-T: 58.4cm/23" - 59cm/23¼"

The **length** is cut at:
Sizes A-G: 53.9cm/21¼"

Sizes H-I: 52.7cm/20¾" - 51.4cm/20¼"

Sizes J-K-L: 50.1cm/19¾" - 48.8cm/19¼" - 47.6cm/18¾"

Sizes M-N-O: 46.3cm/18¼" - 45cm/17¾" - 43.8cm/17¼"

Sizes P-Q-R: 42.5cm/16¾" - 41.2cm/16¼" - 40cm/15¾"

Sizes S-T: 38.7cm/15¼" - 37.4cm/14¾"

✂ Adjust the sleeve length to change the wingspan.

29

Cut two rectangles for the sleeves as per Step 3, page 29.

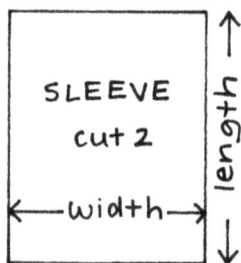

SLEEVE
cut 2
length
width

Sizes G-H-I: 13.9cm/5½" - 14.6cm/5¾" - 15.2cm/6"

Sizes J-K-L: 15.8cm/6¼" - 16.5cm/6½" - 17.1cm/6¾"

Sizes M-N-O: 17.7cm/7" - 18.4cm/7¼" - 19cm/7½"

Sizes P-Q-R: 19.6cm/7¾" - 20.3cm/8" - 20.9cm/8¼"

Sizes S-T: 21.5cm/8½" - 22.2cm/8¾"

Then, lay the rectangles on top of each other *paired*, and measure in from the bottom corner.

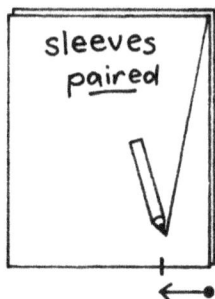

sleeves
paired

The amount to measure is:

Sizes A-B-C: 12cm/4¾" - 12.3cm/4⅞" - 12.7cm/5"

Sizes D-E-F: 13cm/5⅛" - 13.3cm/5¼" - 13.6cm/5⅜"

Rule a line as shown in the diagram, then cut off the wedge. The wedges will be sewn to the opposite sleeves.

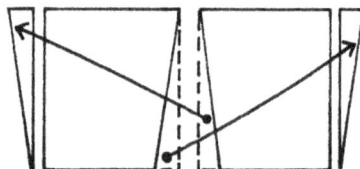

4. Other pieces to cut:

The dimensions can be tweaked to fit your fabric and preference.

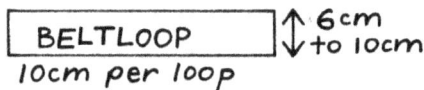

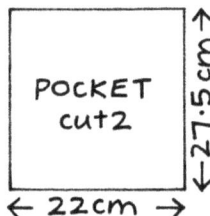

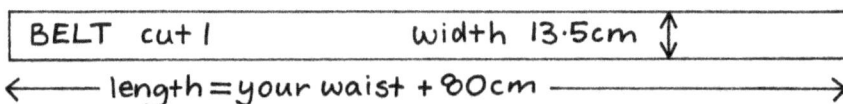

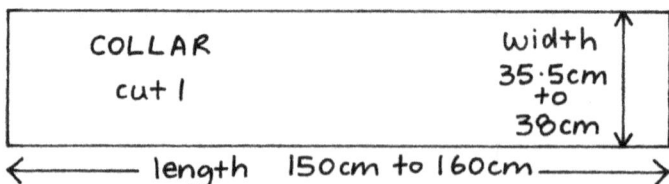

BELTLOOP
10cm per loop
6cm to 10cm

POCKET
cut2
27.5 cm
← 22cm →

BELT cut 1   width 13.5cm
← length = your waist + 80cm →

COLLAR
cut 1
width 35.5cm to 38cm
← length 150cm to 160cm →

Summary of pieces

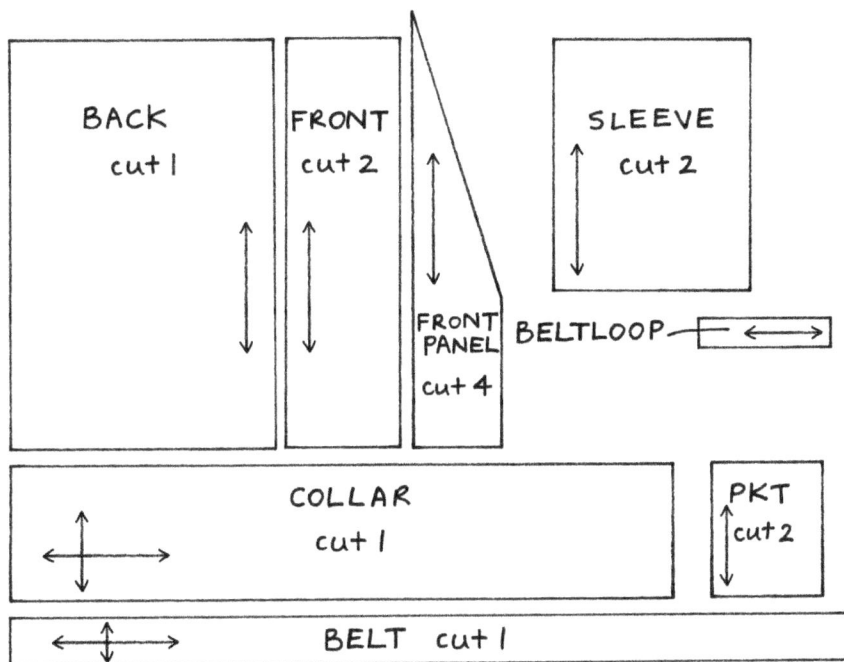

✂ Note the grainlines: the collar and belt can be cut in either direction depending on your fabric and cutting layout.

✂ Consider in-seam pockets instead of patch, if it works better for your design and fabric. Try the zero waste one on page 8.

✂ Do adjust your pieces according to your fabric type.

If you're using very thick fabric such as a woollen blanket or quilted material, you'll need to consider bulk. For example: the collar could be cut as a single layer with bound edges, or the edges left raw if you're using boiled wool. The belt could be simply folded in half longways and the raw edges bound together, or it may look better with no belt. The patch pockets could be stitched on flat with bias binding around the edges, or in-seam pockets used instead. Press seams open instead of to one side.

There's a **1.5cm/⅝" seam allowance** on all pieces and a **4cm/1½" hem allowance** on the sleeves and top edge of the pockets. For easy sewing, **overlock** around the edges of all pieces before starting.

W/S = wrong side, R/S = right side

To sew

1. Sew the shoulder seams, stopping 1.5cm/⅝" each side of the neck. For knits and stretch wovens, stabilise the seam with a strip of fusing or tape.

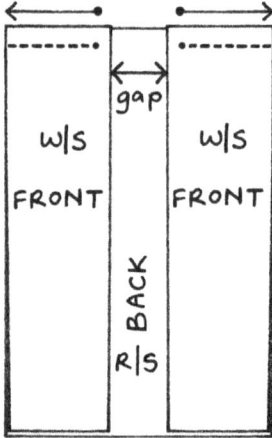

For a more natural shoulder line, angle the seam (recommended).

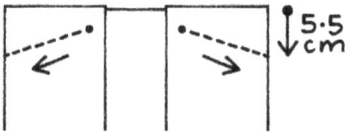

Press the seam open.

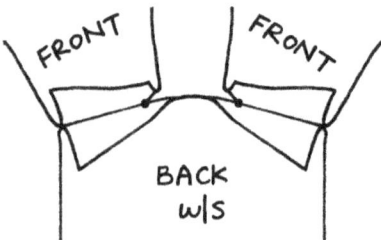

2. Sew the un-interfaced front panels to the fronts.

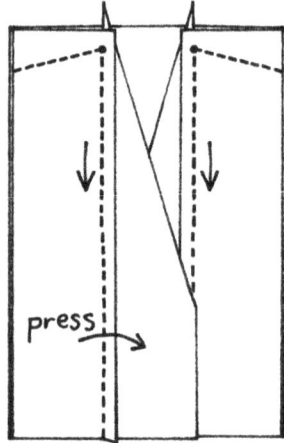

Press the seam towards the centre panel.

3. Sew across the short ends of the collar and turn through. Press.

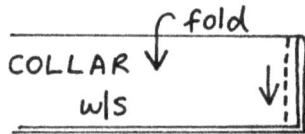

Leave the collar folded like this so it's two thicknesses; you'll be stitching through both layers together in the next two steps.

4. Sew the middle of the collar to the back neck, with the back uppermost and collar underneath.

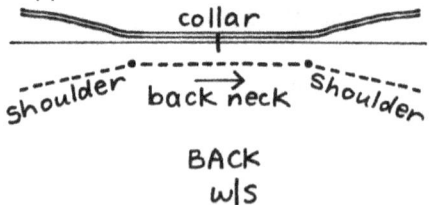

5. Pin the collar onto the fronts.

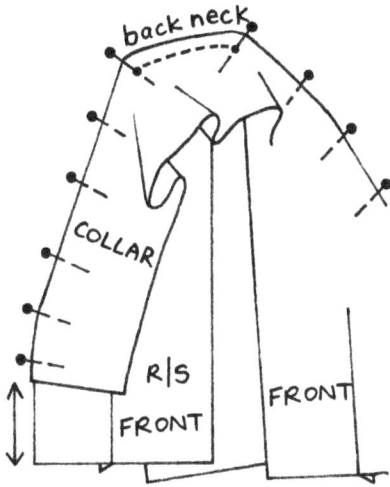

6. Lay the interfaced front panels on top so the collar is sandwiched. Sew. If you know the jacket's length, pivot at the lower corner and sew across on the hemline.

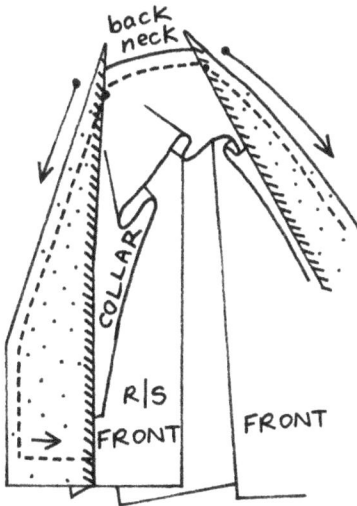

Turn through.
Understitch the front panel.

7. Sew each wedge to its sleeve. Press the seam towards the wedge.

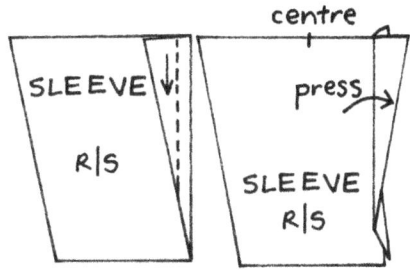

8. Sew the sleeves onto the body, stopping 1.5cm/⅝" short at each end. The wedges can be at the back or front.

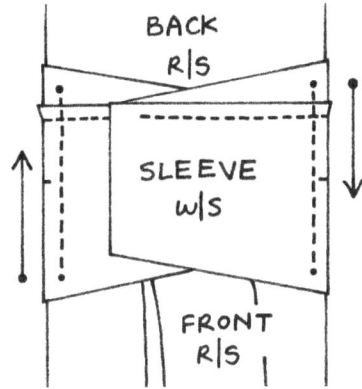

9. Sew the side seam and underarm seam.

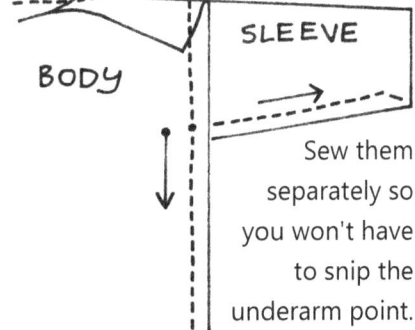

Sew them separately so you won't have to snip the underarm point.

At the wrist, angle the stitching at the hem line.

SLEEVE
w|s

For big sizes, you'll have a section missing due to the sharper angle of the underarm seam:

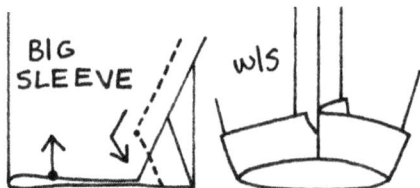
BIG SLEEVE
w|s

10. Make the **patch pockets**.

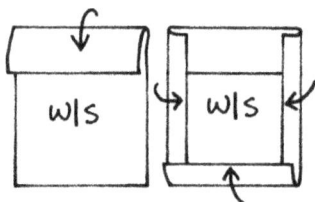
w|s   w|s

When you sew them on, reinforce the corners.

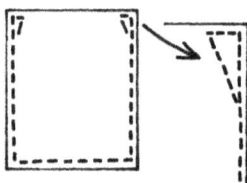

11. Make the **belt**: fold it in half longways and sew the three sides, leaving a gap. Turn through. Press.

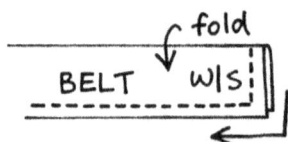
fold
BELT   w|s

12. Sew the **beltloops** as a tube, turn through and sew in place.

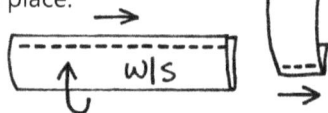
w|s

13. Hem to suit.

Optional: add a lining

A lining can be added before the sleeves are hemmed, or retro-fitted later. This is a free-hanging lining, meaning that the lining isn't joined to the jacket at the hemline. It has the advantage of being easier to iron, easier to alter if needed, and less alarming if either the lining or main fabric shrinks in the wash.

1. Choose a lining fabric. Ideally it should be the same or lighter in weight than the jacket.

It's OK to use a different fabric for the sleeves. For example, you could use a special fabric for the body and a plain one for the sleeves, or a cotton fabric for the body and a slippery one for the sleeves.

2. Cut the front, back and sleeves the same as the jacket, minus the 4cm/1½" hem allowance (why do we cut the hem allowance off? So there's no way the lining will end up longer than the jacket).

```
LINING
BACK
cut 1
```

```
LINING
FRONT
cut 2
```

```
LINING
SLEEVE
cut 2
```

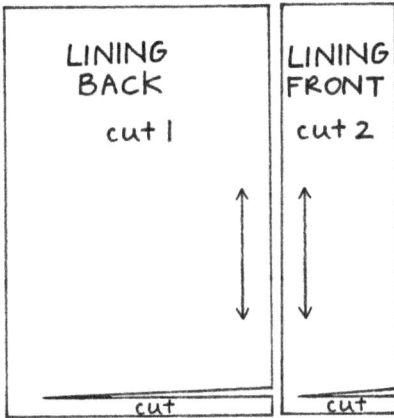

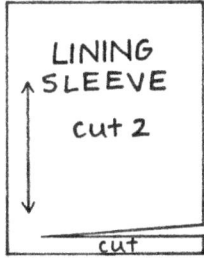

You won't need the centre front panels, because the jacket already has them.

5. Sew the lining to the jacket's back neck and front facing, by hand or machine.

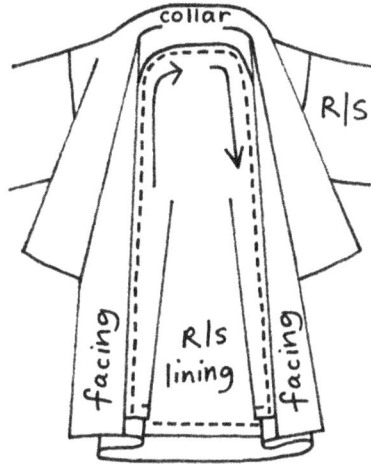

collar

R|S

facing   R|s lining   facing

3. Sew the pieces together the same as the jacket, so you have a (partial) jacket made of lining.

At the wrist, taper the sleeve seam to 6mm/¼".

You can sew the lining with a slightly smaller seam allowance eg 1.2cm/½". It's OK if the lining is a little larger than the jacket, but not smaller.

4. Hem the lower edge of the lining's body.

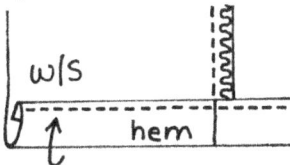

w|s

hem

6. Press up the jacket's sleeve hems, interfacing the hems if req. Attach the lining to the sleeves, taking a 6mm/¼" seam allowance. **Important:** sit the lining inside the jacket, and reach in between them to get to the seam. DO NOT simply put the lining/main right sides together and stitch!

7. Hem the jacket's sleeves, either by hand or machine. If by hand, go back inside the jacket.

8. Optional (but I always do): catch the lining and jacket loosely together at the shoulder points, so the sleeve lining stays put when you take the jacket off.

Birgitta Helmersson, based in Malmö Sweden, designs and develops garments and home sewing patterns using zero waste pattern cutting. She's also the author of *Zero Waste Patterns - 20 projects to sew your own wardrobe* (Quadrille, 2023).

At her studio/store, small collections are sewn in-house using carefully sourced natural fibres along with re-purposed vintage and second-hand textiles. Previously based in Melbourne, Australia, Birgitta has 20 years' experience working as a designer and pattern-maker in both fashion and theatrical costume. Her self titled label was founded in 2013 in Melbourne. Birgitta packed up the business to reconnect with her Swedish roots and re-located to Malmö with her family at the start of 2018.

"From a young age I dreamed of being a designer. My mum bought me a second hand sewing machine when I was 12 and I began teaching myself to make my own clothes. Once I finished school I began to take short courses and skill up in the areas I was interested in, and the rest of my experience I gained by working in the industry. One of my first jobs was in customer service for a clothing alterations company. After several months I managed to convince my boss to allow me to work as a tailor and as they say, the rest is history. Five years later I moved to Melbourne for a job, from my home town of Perth, Western Australia, and spent 10 years working in the fashion and costume industry. It was during this time I started to become interested in zero waste pattern cutting. Back then my experience was that textile waste was very much just accepted as a part of the industry and I really wanted to try and find a way to change this. Many of my roles involved working directly with the designer, who would hand over their sketches to me which I would then develop into patterns and samples. I really loved the problem solving aspect of my work, but I also found it frustrating that there was such a big disconnect between the design and technical aspects of developing a garment.

Since starting my own label in 2013 I have been working with zero waste pattern cutting. I love working this way as I can really combine my love for design and problem solving. When I started there weren't so many resources available to learn about zero waste so it took many years of experimenting to develop patterns that I was happy with, and I did find it extremely challenging at times. I think it is so important to find ways to make zero waste patterns as efficient as possible, which is surprisingly hard to do! If it takes you five times longer to make the garment it sort of defeats the purpose of the whole exercise.

In 2020 I released a sewing pattern alongside one of my collections, the #zwcroppedshirt. I initially thought this would be temporary but it went so well that sewing patterns are now a huge part of what I do, and I absolutely love it. It really opened my eyes to how important it is to actually be able to see how a zero waste design is made to truly be able to understand how it works. This has led to zero waste pattern cutting becoming so much more widely known in recent years. There is a real click moment that comes with using a zero waste pattern for the first time. A little over 10 years ago textile waste was considered 'just a part of the industry', but now I truly believe that this mentality is changing, My hope is that bigger businesses will start to adapt some of these processes to reduce waste, and even eliminate it completely."

www.birgittahelmersson.com   @birgittahelmersson

Ask Lizzy

Q: When making a zero waste pattern, is it "cheating" to use scraps as appliqué?

A: Some people think it is, and others see it as an opportunity for embellishment. Sometimes appliqué is functional, providing an extra layer of fabric for strength - there's a firm historical precedence for this, as it makes clothes stronger and longer-lasting.

I have no problem with appliqué, functional or not, but my own preference is to try and get a layout without it. I try not to use a piece for the sake of not having scraps; every design element and pattern piece should be a functional and integral part of the garment. Each piece should be "strong" with a clear purpose.

Q: What are your thoughts on zero waste and minimal waste?

A: Minimal waste isn't something which should be dismissed as a failure to achieve zero, because minimal waste is still advantageous.

One of the benefits of zero waste patterns is that they're very economical on fabric, often in ways that regular patterns can only dream about. I didn't notice this until I'd made a few zero waste patterns. For years, working as a clothing cutter, I tried to shave centimetres off cutting layouts, and suddenly with zero waste I'm saving tens of centimetres! Although not zero, minimal waste can still save significant amounts of fabric, especially in high volume production, and is part of a path towards change in the fashion industry.

For home sewing pattern designers, calling a pattern "minimal waste" can free you up to create more sizes, some of which may be zero waste and others minimal waste. A minimal waste pattern might be able to be improved on in the future.

April

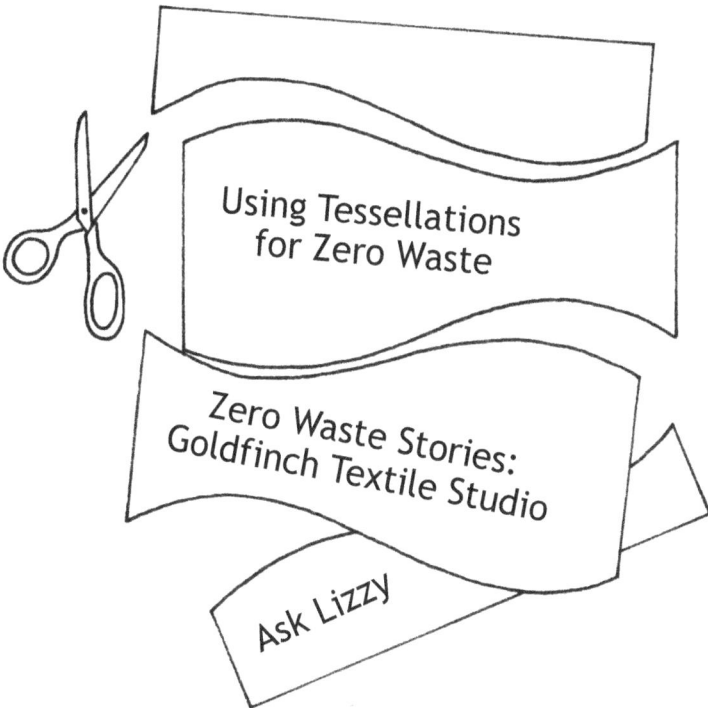

Using Tessellations
for Zero Waste

Zero Waste Stories:
Goldfinch Textile Studio

Ask Lizzy

Using
Tessellations
for zero waste

Tessellating patterns are shapes that fit perfectly into one another with no gaps. You probably have examples of them in your home: patchwork quilts, bathroom tiles, brickwork, honeycomb and jigsaw puzzles are all tessellating patterns. The concept can be used to create pattern pieces for zero waste garments.

First though, here's a brief mathematics textbook theory of tessellations:

1. Take a square and draw a shape on one side. **2.** Cut the shape out and tape it onto the opposite side. **3.** This shape will interlock in a row. **4 & 5.** Take it a step further by repeating the process with the other two sides. **6.** The interlocking shape. You can see that this can give very complex-looking shapes, with curves, with no great effort. In mathematics, this is called a **translation tessellation,** because you only have to slide the shape along to make the tessellated design, rather than having to flip or rotate it.

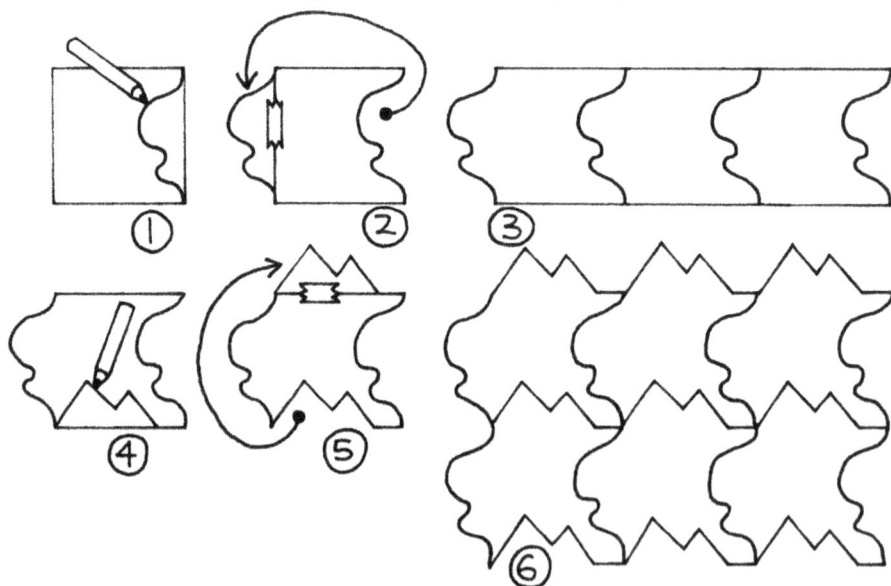

40

flip

Here's another:

1 & 2. Repeat the process, but this time, *flip* the cut-off piece before taping it to the opposite side.

3. The pattern will tessellate with translated and flipped shapes - the shapes marked with an X have been flipped.

This is called a **reflection tessellation**, because the flipped shape looks like a mirror image of the original.

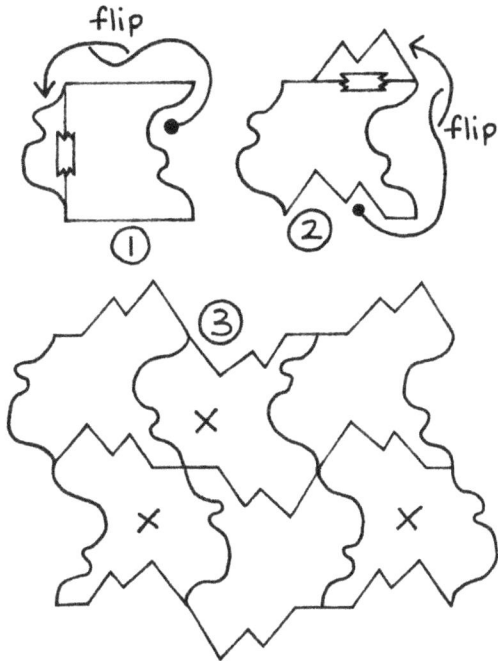

And another...

1 & 2. Repeat the process one more time, but move the cut-off piece to the *adjacent side*. **3.** The piece has to be turned around a point to create the tessellating pattern. This is called a **rotation tessellation** because, obviously, the piece is rotated.

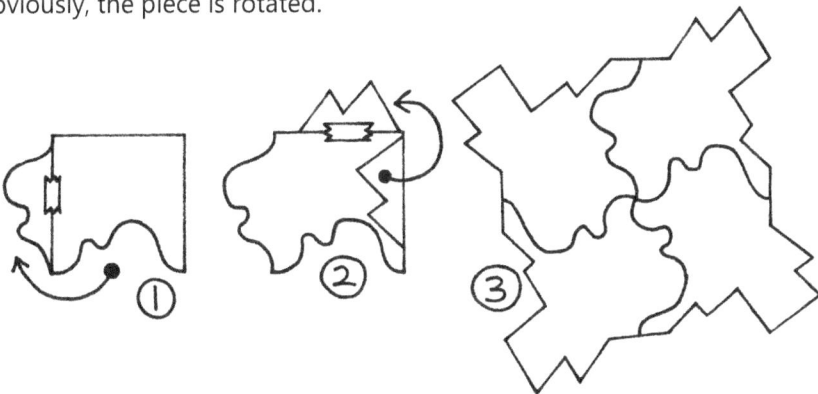

Using tessellations for zero waste patterns

The basis for a tessellating shape doesn't have to be a square - it can be any shape which naturally tessellates, such as one of these:

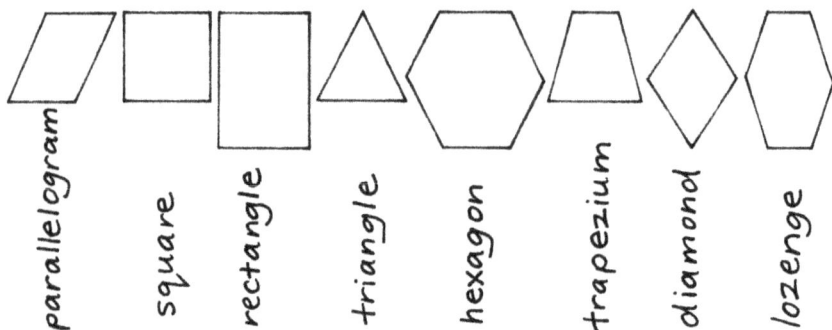

parallelogram   square   rectangle   triangle   hexagon   trapezium   diamond   lozenge

Any of these can be used as a garment pattern piece on its own, too.

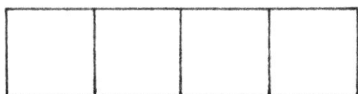

Squares and rectangles will form a row of pattern with no waste around the edges.

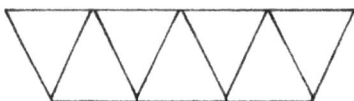

Triangles and trapeziums will form rows if they're top-and-tailed. This means *it only works for 2-way fabrics, **not** napped or directional prints.*

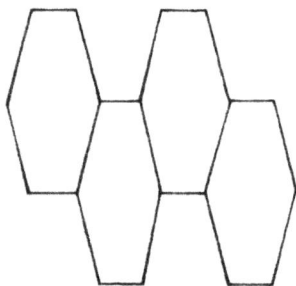

Diamonds and lozenges will fit together off-set with a half-drop. There will be spare fabric around the edges on all sides.

Trapeziums are one of my favourite shapes because they're so versatile.

A trapezium can form the front and back of an A-line skirt, or any number of skirt gores.

SKIRT BACK

SKIRT FRONT

A trapezium also makes a good tapered drop-shouldered sleeve.

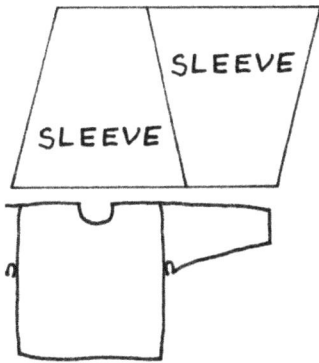

Or it can be the basis for a sleeve with more shape.

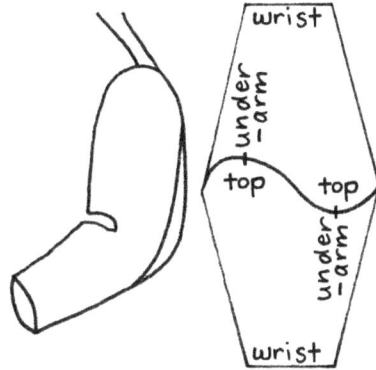

Most often when I use tessellations, I **tessellate** *one complete side* **of a pattern piece.**

Here's an example of a tunic/dress/coat pattern. **1.** Draw a shape on *half* of one side. I've started with a rectangle and drawn the sleeve and underarm curve. **2.** Pivot the shape around on point A so that the lower half now has the opposite curve. **3.** The resulting shape can be top-and-tailed with itself. A quirk is that the sleeves will get longer as the sizes get bigger. **4.** The finished garment looks a bit like this.

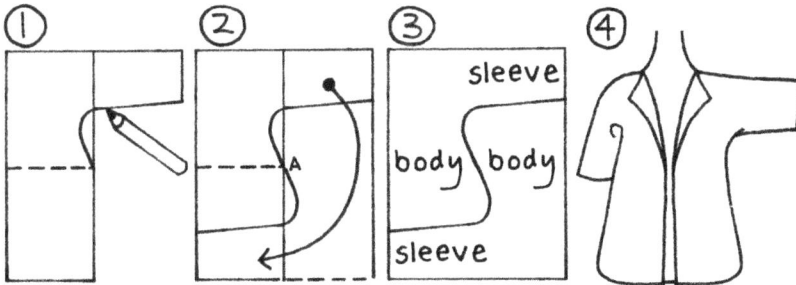

Two important things to note:

1. For any shapes with curves you'll need to have **the seam allowances already on the piece** you're tessellating. You need the *final shape*, because addding them afterwards changes the outline and the curves won't fit back together. This is potentially difficult if you're using computer software which only lets you add the seam allowances *after* you've done the patternmaking.

2. This tessellating process **doesn't create a pair** - it's the same shape rotated. If you need a pair of shapes, either cut a second one flipped, or put two layers of fabric right sides together when you cut it out.

The tunic/dress/coat pattern example can be used in a few different ways:

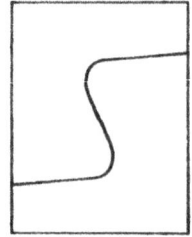

✂ You can leave it like it is and have a central seam in the front and back. This gives you a convenient rectangular unit with no wasted space around the edges.

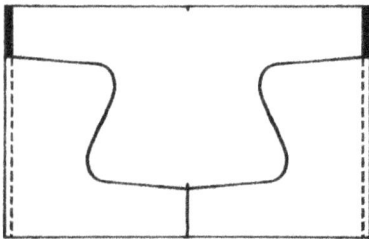

✂ You could mirror the tessellated block to give you one seamless piece and another with a central seam. This gives a tiny amount of waste on one set of sleeves (a seam allowance's worth - the shaded area) which might be handy for something else.

✂ You could mirror the shape so you have no central seams. Being tessellated it could continue infinitely, but the fabric *isn't* infinite so you would have waste at each end.

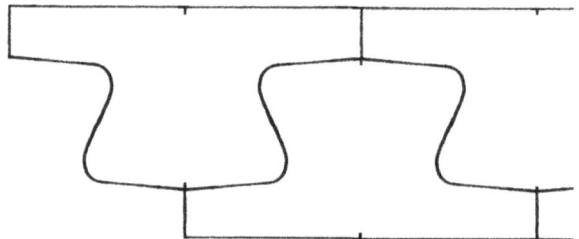

But you could put half-shapes at each end.

If you can manage it, it's advantageous to have straight sides on the edges of a tessellated piece, making it modular, because (as we will see more about on page 47) it prevents wastage at the sides of the fabric. This might mean using a central seam in the garment.

Here's another way I use to make tessellated pieces. It uses flipping rather than pivoting. This example makes an apron shaped piece.

1. Draw the shape on *half* of one side. **2 & 3.** Flip the shape and draw it onto the other half. **4.** Mirror the piece if required. **5.** The finished garment. **6.** This creates a tessellation with a half-drop. Notice that the shape can be made wider or narrower without affecting the tessellation.

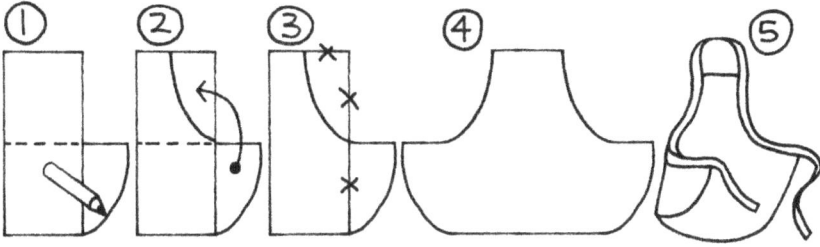

Half-drop tessellations don't sit neatly in rectangular fabric - there's an odd outline and waste fabric around the edges.

I suggest only using them for small pattern pieces where lots are required (thus minimizing the percentage of waste), or finding a solution for the fabric around the edges.

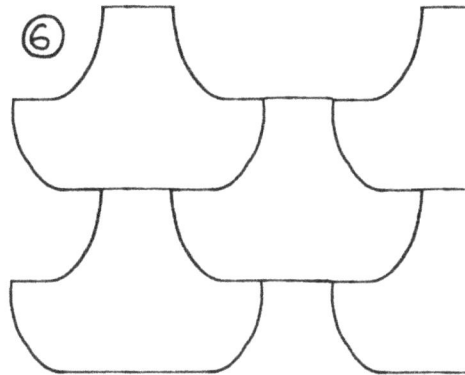

Ways to use tessellated patterns

Tessellating pieces are a good solution for **small pieces/garments that you want to cut multiples of**, for example gussets, underwear pieces, patchwork quilt pieces, baby clothes, accessories and bags.

You can tessellate a single garment piece with itself or a whole garment nested together (if you can contain all the pieces within a tessellate-able shape).

One way of working is to create each pattern piece so that it nests into itself and can be marked out in rows on the fabric from selvedge to selvedge. The number of garments to be cut depends on the lowest common denominator of pattern pieces.

For example, say we need one of each of these pieces per garment - a curved shape and a trapezium.
The fabric width will allow 5 curved pieces and 4 trapeziums to be marked across.

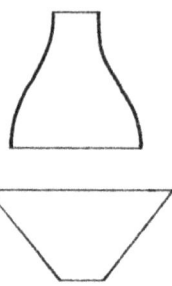

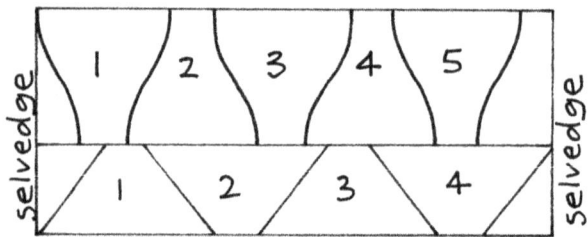

The smallest number of whole garments you can cut is therefore 20 (because 20 is the smallest number that is divisible by both 5 and 4). We would need to mark out 4 rows of curved shapes and 5 rows of trapeziums.

What if you can't make a piece tessellate with itself?

Consider combining it with another shape/s to fill in the gap. The pieces together form the repeating unit. For example, this front pattern piece for underpants could be marked across the fabric like this, and the negative shapes in between used for part of the back or a different garment.

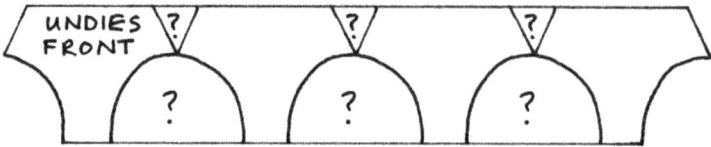

Here's another way you could do it, giving you a bigger, and possibly easier, shape to use.

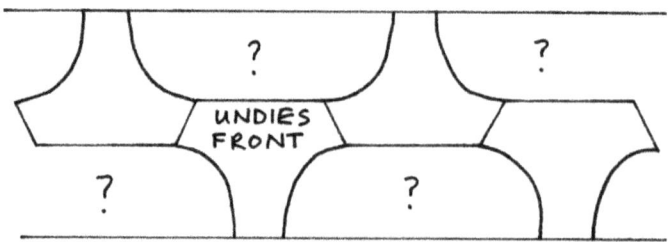

How about the bits on the edges?

Tessellations, unless they're square/rectangular and occur in a row, will inevitably leave you with half-shapes at the sides and ends. This waste can really add up, alongside the selvedges in particular. At each cut end, the waste will be a smaller percentage overall the more you cut (in other words, a long cutting table is an asset).

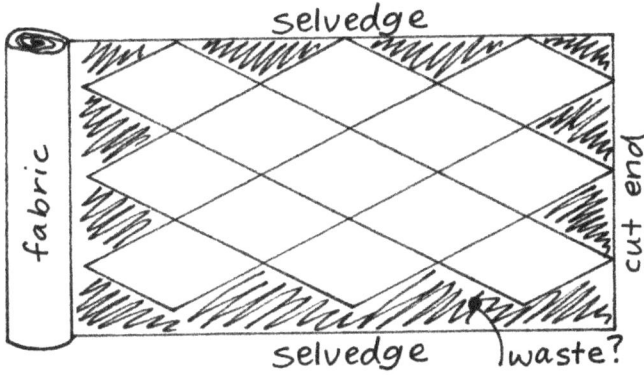

If you don't address this, you might end up wasting more fabric via the edges than you're saving in the middle. This is why it's advantageous to have straight sides on tessellating pieces, but it's not always possible.

Here are some ideas:

✂ Often the space left at the sides of a layout can be seamed together to make a whole piece if a seam allowance is added. This means some garments will have a seam and some won't.

✂ Can you fit other pattern pieces into the wasted space? Maybe even for a different garment?

✂ Sometimes this works in your favour, for example, a gored skirt like this, which needs a centre back seam, or a wraparound skirt which needs straight ends. You might achieve no waste by mixing-and-matching sizes to fit the pieces perfectly across the fabric, or you might be able to tweak pieces by changing the width of a centre back seam, the depth of a pleat etc.

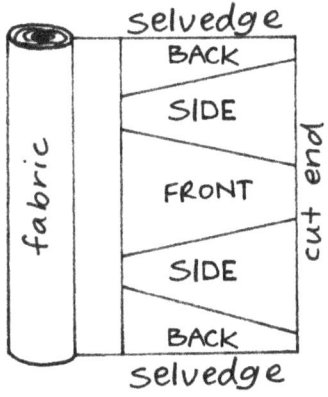

47

goldfinch
textile studio

Emily Klug owns **Goldfinch Textile Studio**, which focuses on creating minimal/zero-waste patterns for the home sewist and finding creative ways to utilize reclaimed and upcycled materials. Emily has been garment sewing for over 12 years and has a background in architecture and lighting design. She is based in Wisconsin, USA.

Her minimal/zero-waste sewing patterns are designed to maximize the use of the required fabric resulting in a garment that is both modern and timeless. They are designed for flexibility and adaptability, allowing the sewist to create something uniquely their own.

"Designing zero-waste patterns came as a natural progression in my making journey. After spending many years exploring ways to use upcycled materials and fabric cutoffs to create new garments, I was ready to investigate ways to eliminate this waste from the start. When I began to learn about zero-waste pattern cutting, I knew I had found an avenue that I wanted to explore more.

My background in architecture lends itself nicely to zero waste pattern design. Much like when working on a floor plan, a zero-waste pattern layout requires figuring out the best way all the pieces will work together to create a harmonious outcome - a wearable garment. The task of making this puzzle work is the part of zero-waste design that I find the most challenging and most rewarding. You have a set of limits from the get-go that help to define the direction of your design. These limits are both restrictive and surprisingly freeing.

My goal is to design garments for everyday wear, with a focus on details that create an elevated basic. Much of my work starts with a general idea of what type of garment I would like to design. Then working in Illustrator, I begin to break down the garment into the pieces that could be used to become the final garment. There is a lot of give and take to get all the parts to work as a whole. Once I have achieved a workable layout, I take the design to fabric. This could be a full scale toile or a ¼ scale mock-up. I like to test wear the garment to see what needs potential tweaking. If changes need to be made, I go back to the pattern layout and make adjustments.

When I am designing a pattern, I'm always thinking about how the pattern can be graded up and down to create as many sizes as possible. If a pattern layout only works for one size, then I go back and adjust to find something that is more flexible. Another way to get more sizes is to offer slightly different pattern layouts for different size groups. This has worked well for me, as I can adjust the layout to accommodate the needs of various sizes.

One of the more difficult things about zero-waste design is communicating the non-traditional methods of pattern cutting and sewing to the home sewist. It can be a bit tricky to wrap your brain around how a pattern layout can be transformed into a garment. I have found that mini-models (paper or fabric) and video are very helpful in communicating how the pattern pieces come together. I want people to see that there is more to zero-waste design than just "un-wearable futuristic garments or oversized sacks". By exploring and pushing the design process, I hope to convey the depth of possibilities available within zero-waste design."

Ask Lizzy

Q: Lizzy, can you pick a garment that's zero waste?

A: Up until now (April 2022), I would say almost always yes. There are a few dead giveaways. For example, anything based on a bog coat cutting concept will have a cross-chest or cross-back seam. Fitted sleeves which have the sleeve heads nesting into themselves will always have a seam running down the outside length from shoulder to wrist. Many are an easy-fitting aesthetic with few curves, possibly based on traditional shapes, especially from designers new to zero waste (including myself early on). However, patterncutters are getting more confident and experienced with zero waste and it's getting way more difficult to tell the difference.

Q: When grading zero waste patterns, should large sizes be exactly like small sizes or is it okay to vary the design as you grade up?

A: In an ideal world, yes, all the sizes would be an identical design, but there's a chasm of difference between an 86cm/34" bust and a 178cm/70" bust, not just in size but in shape and proportions. Occasionally it's possible to make all the sizes an identical design, but not always. My own view is that as long as the customer clearly knows what they're getting, it's fine to have small differences - another reason for showing a variety of sizes on a variety of models.

There are going to *have* to be differences for reasons of fit. For example, after around a 127cm/50" waist, a waistband will struggle to stay up - it needs to be replaced by an elastic waist or at least elastic at the back. A larger size will require bust darts so that the front hem stays level, whereas it may be okay not to have any for smaller sizes. With zero waste, the fabric width has a bearing on how the pieces will fit back on, and sometimes an extra seam or two is needed to fit on the fabric with no waste.

May

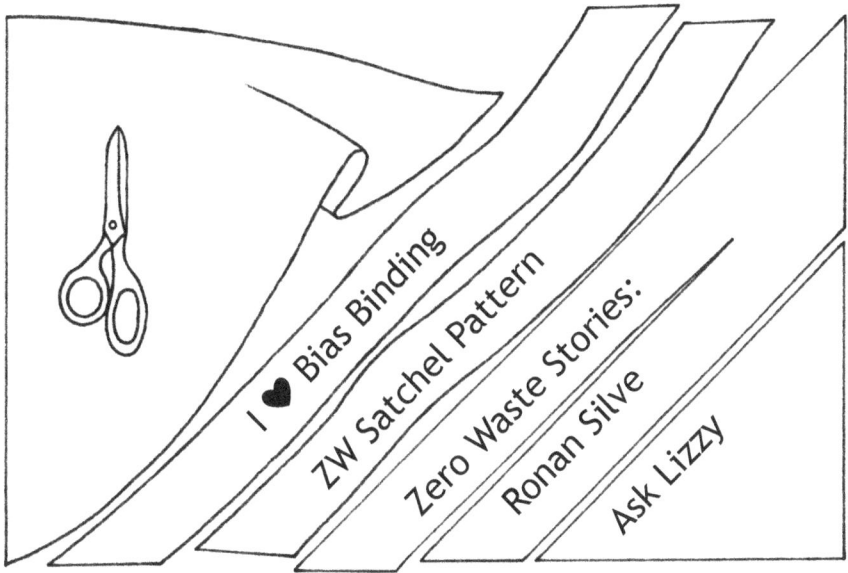

I ♥ Bias Binding

ZW Satchel Pattern

Zero Waste Stories:

Ronan Silve

Ask Lizzy

I ♥ Bias Binding

Bias binding is something I find myself using again and again in zero waste garments, both to actually bind an edge or use as a facing. The big attraction is, of course, that no extra fabric needs to be found in the layout for finishing off the edges, for example, with regular facings.

There are many other things to love about bias binding: the neat finish inside-and-out, an elegant solution to bulky edges, the chance to use a contrasting fabric, the flexibility of the bias and the way it smoothly hugs curves with no ripples or pleats, as a beautiful finish for fine and transparent fabrics...I could go on...and on...

It's interesting that historical clothes appear to use binding cut on the *straight* grain, rather than the bias. Makers used strips of fabric to stabilise and cover the raw edge.

Why the straight and not the bias? Possibly cutting on the bias was considered too wasteful, and it can be difficult if you have narrow fabric widths. Cutting binding on the straight grain is easier to do and it's easier to calculate lengths needed. The straight grain keeps edges from stretching.

They managed it because the binding tended to be narrow and seams were finer, so there was a better chance of it sitting flat around curves. As clothes were sewn entirely by hand, they had more control and could manipulate the fabric as they sewed around curves. The wool and linen they used were pliable and able to be shaped better than most cotton and synthetics.

However, modern-day quilters, who use binding around the edges of their quilts, attest that binding cut on the *bias* is more durable than the straight grain. The theory is that straight grain binding creates a weaker edge because the fold lines up with only one (or a few) threads on the grain of the fabric. If that one thread goes, the entire edge goes. The bound edge of a quilt receives the roughest treatment - for example, if the quilt lies on a bed and hits the ground, or if the person sleeping under the quilt has a beard (the whiskers abrade the fabric; it also happens on sheets). Handling, washing and folding also creates wear on the edges, much as it does for clothes. Binding cut on the *bias* puts the fold on the cross-section of the weave, so the multiple threads lie diagonally and cross over the folded edge. If one thread wears out, the binding will still be intact.

Let's go back to historical clothes for a moment:
Does binding cut on the bias *really* use more fabric than if it's cut on the straight grain? Nope, because the surface area is the same, but there will be more joins if it's bias cut (so maybe it does, if we count the extra seams used for the joins, or waste if the joins are avoided).
Is it wasteful? Yes—if you only require a single or few strips. Then you're left with the two triangles from each side of the strip. The attraction of straight grain strips is that they can be conveniently cut as-needed in any quantity from any rectangle. For bias strips, you really need to cut up a whole square/rectangle and use it all to avoid waste, but this is practical if your use is ongoing.

Making and using bias binding
I use both purchased and home-made bias binding. If I don't already have or can't buy what I need, I make it using (preferably) fabric I already have.

To make bias binding, you'll need strips of fabric cut on the bias, typically 2.5cm/1" wide strips for 1.2cm/½" bias binding and 5cm/2" for 2.5cm/1" binding. If the fabric is fine and flimsy, the strips may need to be slightly wider to counteract the narrowing caused by bias drop.
What's the best way to do this? Ideally, we want zero waste, with minimal joins, easy and fast to do. There are two approaches to cutting strips: joining the strips before cutting and joining them afterwards.

Cutting un-joined strips, zero waste

This is how I cut strips when I was a cutter in a corporate uniform factory. In the factory, we aimed to cut strips at maximum length, so there were as few joins as possible. Usually the fabric was fairly stable, eg poly/cotton poplin. I would chalk out strips straight onto the fabric, using a set square to find the 45 degree angle and a long ruler for the lines. I chalked strips for about 50cm-60cm, forming a parallelogram, then I cut it off and cut more parallelograms the same size from the roll. I laid these up, put the end triangle in there too, and cut through all the layers with a machine. As there was an ongoing need for bias strips for piping and bias binding, any spares got used later.

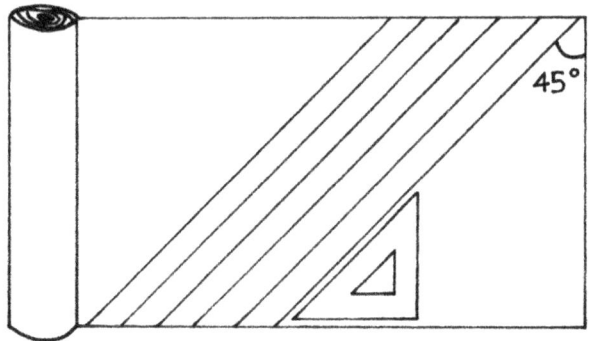

This is actually how I cut them at home too, but I don't need as many! But I try for long lengths, few joins, and I keep spare strips in the offcuts box.

I use scissors but it's easy to cut it this way with a rotary cutter and mat - the mats have 45 degree lines to follow.

Cutting pre-joined strips, zero waste

1. Start with a perfect square and cut it in half diagonally to give two triangles. **2.** Place the triangles right sides together as shown. Sew with a 6mm/¼" seam, using a small stitch length eg 1.5. Match the edges at the *seamline*, not the cut edges. **3.** Press the seam open - you now have a parallelogram. Mark the strips parallel to the longest edge. Cut off any part-strips when you get to the end. **4 & 5.** Fold the fabric into a tube, one strip offset, matching the marked strips. Sew with a 6mm/¼" seam and a small stitch length. Press open. **6.** Cut along the marked lines - you'll cut around and around in one continuous cut.

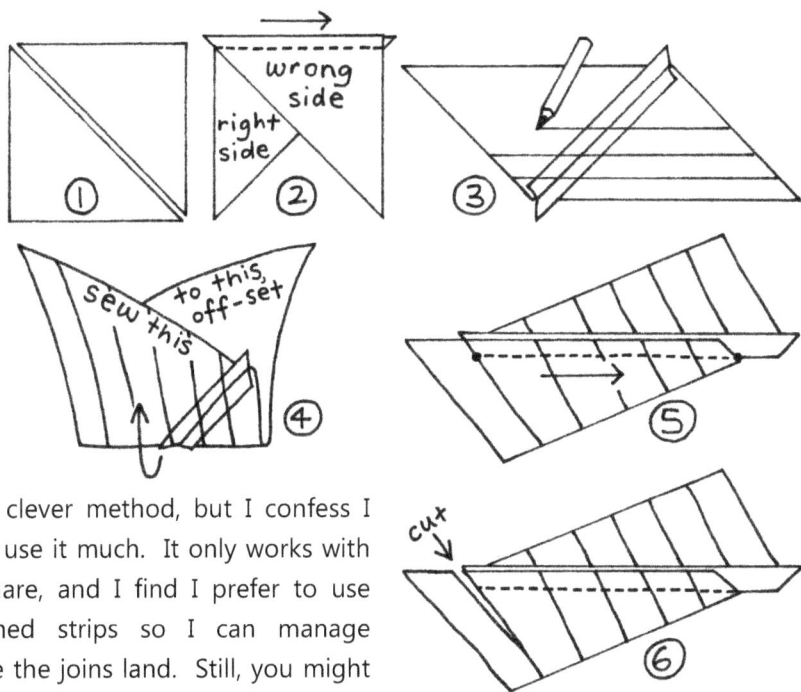

It's a clever method, but I confess I don't use it much. It only works with a square, and I find I prefer to use unjoined strips so I can manage where the joins land. Still, you might find it works well for you.

✂ If you have a *rectangle* to start with, you can form a parallelogram using the step-by-step method on page 103, then mark in the strips as above.

Clothing factories sometimes use pre-joined strips. In a different factory, making sports uniforms, we had an ancient-looking machine to cut knit fabric into strips. It worked like an overlocker without the sewing part. The machinist took a large length of fabric and sewed the selvedges together to make a tube, offset by one strip width (the strips were cut across the fabric, not on the bias). She would feed it throught the machine which would cut the strip and wind it onto a spool, ready for the binding machine.

After cutting strips, and if the fabric is stable, I run them through a bias binding tool to create the folds. For flimsy fabrics, I don't use a tool; I fold the binding as I apply it. For wider binding, if it doesn't flow through a tool properly, I revert to Plan B: I iron the strip in half, longways, then press one edge to the centre. I sew the unpressed edge to the garment first.

10 binding tips for a superior finish

1. Binding is applied in a **two-stage operation**: it's sewn to one side, then brought over to hide the raw edge and stitched down.

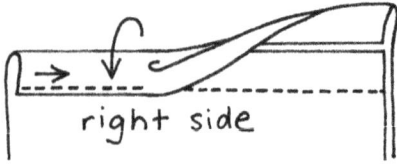

right side

wrong side

Sew the binding to the *wrong side first* if you're going to **machine stitch it on the right side**. Ideally sew the first row in a thread which matches the *garment*.

OR

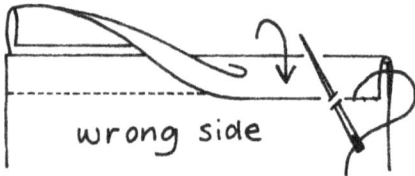

For an invisible finish, sew the binding to the *right side first* then bring it over to the **wrong side and hand sew** it in place.

2. Sew the binding on so that it **fully encases the raw edge**. If you sew it half on, you'll get a ridge when you press it.

3. Join bias binding by stitching on the *straight grain*. Trim and press open.

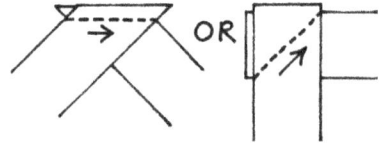

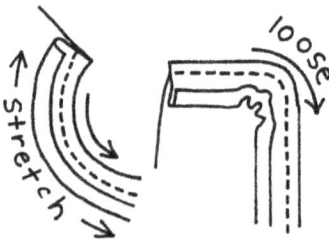

OR

4. For **concave curves** (underarms, necklines etc) slightly stretch the binding as you sew it on. For **convex curves** (eg outward corners) sew it a little looser around the curve.

stretch

loose

5. For neat ends, wrap the binding around the end when you sew the first row, and stitch through all the layers. Fold it in place for the second row.

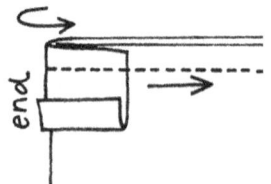

end

6. To bind corners: 1. Sew the binding until you reach the exact point where the seam lines cross. Backstitch and lift the needle from the fabric. **2.** Diagonally fold the binding *away* from the corner. **3.** Fold the binding straight back so the fold is aligned with the binding's *raw edge* (**not** the previous stitching line). Stitch along the binding. **4 & 5.** Fold the binding over to the other side, at the same time forming a mitre on the corner.

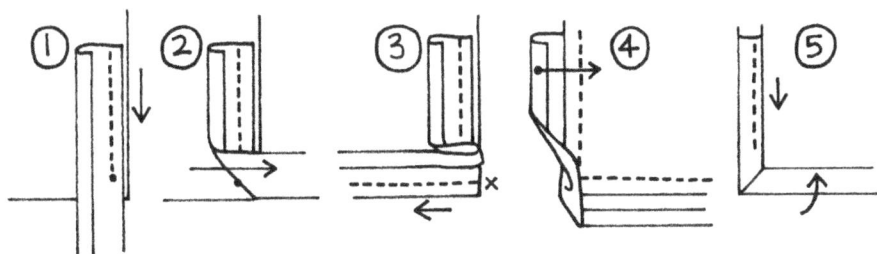

7. Old neckties are very handy for making small amount of bias binding.

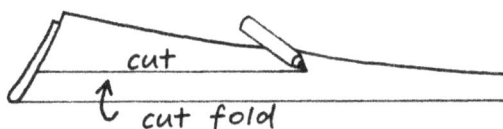

Unpick it and save the interfacing to recycle into a new tie. Press the fabric in half longways and slit the fold, then cut the tie into strips. Even ugly neckties can make beautiful binding (or piping, rouleau, ties or loops).

8. Use your iron. It takes more time if you press each step of applying the binding but it makes it easier to sew and therefore gives you better results.

9. If you're making a **bias cut garment**, any extra length you cut off the bottom can be used for bias binding.

10. Does your bias binding **ripple** after it's sewn? Especially if it's applied by machine?

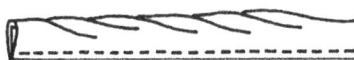

Thoughts: ✂ This can happen if the binding isn't cut on the true bias.
✂ Sometimes it helps to iron the binding in half before you start sewing.
✂ Try using a walking foot, if you have one. ✂ For the final row of machine sewing, hold the underneath layer (the garment) firmly with your left hand, pulling it forward, and let the binding "sit easy" on top as you stitch.

Make a Zero Waste Satchel

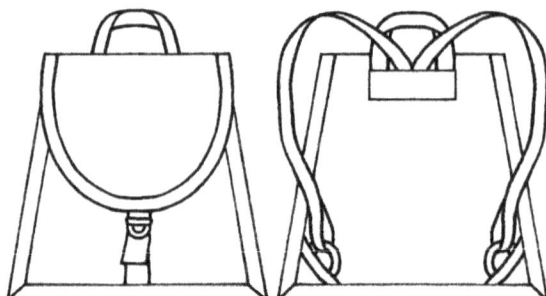

This little handbag-sized satchel has two interior pockets, a gusset and backpack straps. It's practically a tribute to bias binding - every seam and edge has it.

Finished size: 23cm/9" wide x 21cm/8¼" high.

A sew-a-long is on YouTube: www.youtube.com/watch?v=dV30V0ah6rs

You need:

✂ Sturdy fabric such as denim, upholstery fabric, corduroy, canvas or firmly woven wool. Optional: interfacing and lining.

✂ Bias binding: 1.30m/52" of 1.2cm/½" & 3m/119" of 2.5cm/1".

✂ Sewing thread to match the fabric and binding.

✂ 4 D-rings, 2.5cm/1" or 2cm/¾".

Make a pattern

1. Front. Draw a trapezium 21cm/8¼" high, 18cm/7" wide across the top and 23cm/9" across the bottom. Cut 1.

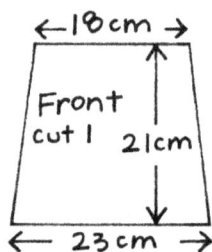

←18cm→
Front
cut 1   21cm
← 23cm →

2. Gusset/pocket. Trace around the front. Draw in a U-shape, straight for 12.5cm/5" and curved at the bottom. Cut 2.

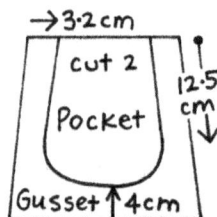

→3.2cm
cut 2
Pocket   12.5 cm
Gusset ↑4cm

3. Back/flap/details. Trace the front twice, joined at the short edge. Rule a horizontal line 5cm/2" up from the bottom. This strip is for the strap attachment. Draw a curved line as shown, 3.5cm/1⅜" in from each corner. These triangle-y parts will become the lower attach points for the backpack straps. Cut 1.

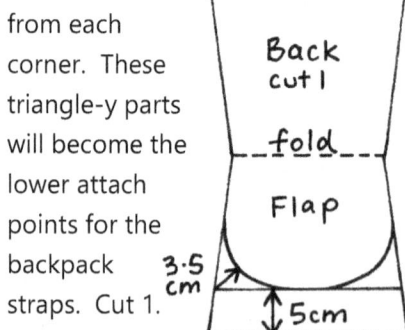

Back
cut 1
__fold__
Flap
3.5 cm   ↕5cm

58

To Cut

The main fabric pieces are all trapeziums and fit together. If you have a selvedge on the fabric, you can cut a piece in half and create a central seam, as shown here.
Cut the lining and/or interfacing with the same layout.

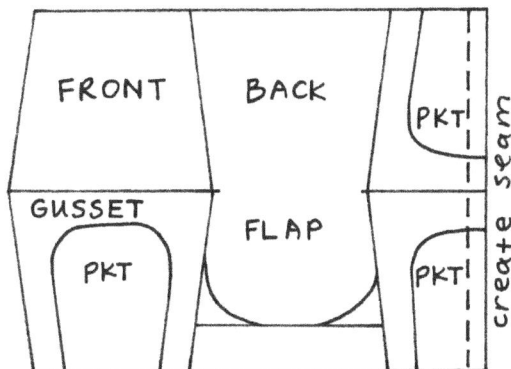

(single layer of fabric)

You also need to cut (not necessarily in the same fabric):

✂ 2 straps 1.5cm/⅝"-2.5cm/1" wide *finished* and each at least 63cm/25" long for children and 76cm/30" for slim adults.

✂ 1 handle for the top, 23cm/9" long and the same width as the straps.

✂ Tabs 15cm/6" & 7.5cm/3" long to fit the width of the D-rings for the front closure.

To Sew

All references to "binding" mean 2.5cm/1" binding unless stated.
R/S and W/S = right side and wrong side of fabric.

1. Prepare the two patch pockets. Bind the top edge.

2. Use an iron to shape 1.2cm/½" binding around the edge, half-lapped over. Leave 2cm/¾" hanging over at each end.

Sew the binding to the pocket on the *inner* edge. Do this for both pockets.

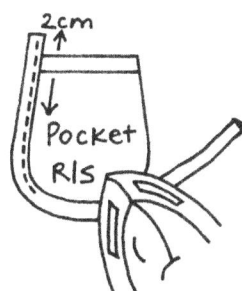

3. Front. Lay one pocket on the W/S of the front (or the R/S of the front lining, if you're lining the bag),

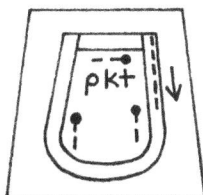

59

centred top and bottom.
Tuck the 2cm/¾" lengths of binding under at the top. Sew around the *outer* edge of the binding, reinforcing the corners.

4. Lay the front and front lining together, W/S matching. Bind the top.

Baste the rest of the lining to the front around the edges.

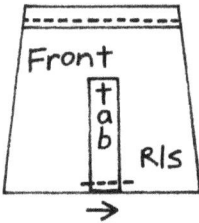

Baste the 15cm/ 6" front closure tab to the bottom edge.

5. Gussets.
If lining the gussets, baste the pieces together now and treat it as one unit.

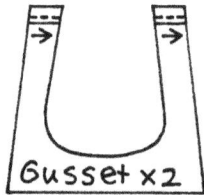

Bind the 4 tops of the gussets.

6. Lay the two gussets R/S together and bind the curve, finishing the tops neatly.

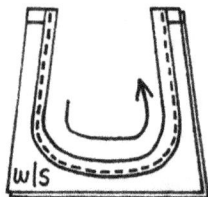

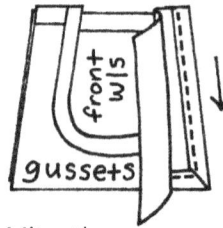

7. Place one gusset edge on the front, W/S together, and bind.

Mitre the corners and finish the tops neatly.

8. Back. Take the two triangle-y pieces and sew a 12.5cm/5" length of 1.2cm/½" binding to the curved edge, flat - the same way as you did for the pockets in Step 2.

9. Take the long rectangular piece and cut 5cm/2" off each end.
On the *middle section*, press 1cm/ ⅜" under on each side. This will be used to anchor the straps at the top of the bag.
On the *two end pieces*, press under each side and stitch, making a tab to fit the width of your D-rings. Slip each tab through a ring. These will be used to attach the straps at the bottom corners.

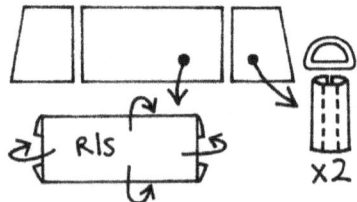

10. Tuck a **tabbed D-ring** from Step 9 under the binding on each triangle and sew to each lower corner of the back.

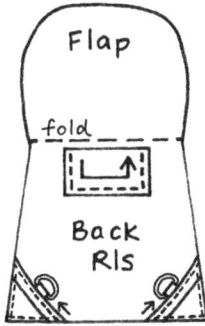

Position the **rectangular piece** from Step 9 6mm/¼" down from the fold line. Edgestitch, leaving the top edge unstitched to insert the straps later.

11. Sew the remaining prepared pocket to the W/S of the back (or R/S of the back lining if you have a lining), same as you did for the front. The pocket should clear the rectangular strap holder.

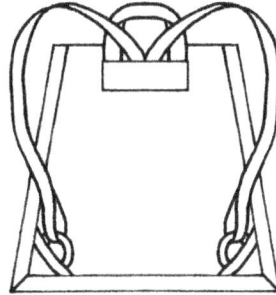

12. If the bag has a lining, lay the back and back lining W/S together and baste around the edges.

Lay the back and remaining gusset W/S together and bind around the edge.

Mitre the corners and begin and end the binding at the lower centre back.

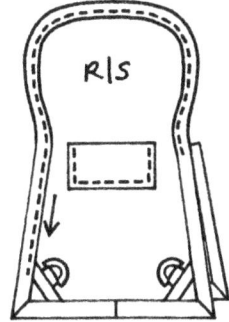

13. On the back, add straps and a handle to suit the wearer - tuck the ends into the open top of the rectangle and stitch. Thread the lower end of the straps through the D-rings and stitch.

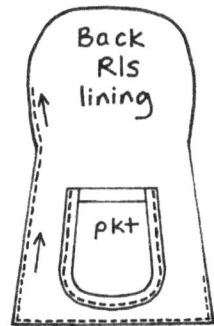

On the front, slip the remaining 7.5cm/3" long tab through 2 D-rings and sew it to the bag's flap.

61

D E I S

Passionate about garment creation and construction, France-based designer **Ronan Silve** creates zero waste garment patterns for menswear, offering designs with a rugged workwear aesthetic and interesting details.

At the beginning, he wanted to be self employed by selling finished garments online but he didn't want to sell garments that people didn't need. He looked for a point of difference for his designs, an eco-conscious aspect to make his garments different from the billions of others sold in stores.

"At the beginning, I got into fashion because I have never found something "different" for men in French stores. Indeed, men's state of mind and social representation are not as free as women's ones are. After studying at horticulture school, I decided to come into fashion, and started a fashion degree because I wanted to change that. This is why my work specializes in menswear. Many years later, my assessment of menswear remains unchanged; especially in zero waste, menswear offerings are not rich.

I got started with zero waste design because I wanted to be self-employed and create in an eco- conscious way but I didn't know how to. Everything changed when I met Mylène L'Orguilloux of www.reformonsnous.fr at a workshop she led for the company I was working for. She explained to us what zero waste design is and presented different paths to experiment and discover it. The workshop deeply unlocked my brain about this design method. Since that moment, I have enjoyed the multidisciplinary approach of zero waste and I

62

decided not to sell finished garments anymore.

Today, my main activity consists in creating patterns especially for menswear. I try to come up with garments that look conventional, to invite men to wear them. This is the first step to show that zero waste for men can be easily wearable. However, as the relationship between men, fashion and their masculinity is evolving, I hope to create garments more conceptual and creative, even more extravagant.

To bring about a new garment, I think about what kind of wardrobe piece I want to create. Then, I look for inspiration, which is in the workers, sailors and railway workers sphere. I draft some ideas, silhouettes or details I like, and quickly start to work on CLO 3D. I build a garment base with the final fit I would like. Then I cut the pattern pieces and turn them until I find a trail leading me to a zero waste garment. In order to limit the fabric consumption, I build a 3D simulation, which helps me realize the final look and fit of the garment. Then, before I cut a full-scale prototype, I make a half-scale prototype that I put on a miniature dummy model. This step is very useful to identify problems. However, each pattern I've designed, I've faced a reluctant piece I didn't known how to place. When I'm stuck with an area of waste I don't know what to do with, I ask myself *What do we need when we wear it? What need must this garment cover?* For most of the time, this method helps me find a consistent answer. Indeed, questioning the mood of the garment is a good way not to use pieces as an embellishment.

Nevertheless, my zero waste designer activity does not allow me to earn a living and I frequently wonder what kind of future is possible for zero waste design. On a personal view, I think about how to face the challenges of having a zero waste brand - how to earn money to live and make my brand viable is important. Globally, I think zero waste must be integrated by the big brands in their processes to reduce the fabric consumption. Despite the fact that zero waste cannot be applied to every garment, it may be an answer to fabric waste in the industry. I think the answer must be sought in industry because big brands have the means to make change. Moreover, zero waste and profits are not incompatible."

www.maisondeis.fr   @deis_officiel

Ask Lizzy

Q: Why are zero waste patterns boxy and voluminous?

A: Some are and some aren't. The designer might want a boxy and volumious aesthetic. Or maybe the designer found it easier to do zero waste.   Obviously, it's much easier to use boxy square shapes because the fabric is square, and voluminous clothes fit more bodies so there's less to worry about with sizing. However, not all zero waste patterns are boxy and voluminous - some use curved shapes very cleverly - and as patternmakers get more practiced with this way of making patterns we can expect to see more complex pattern cutting. Modern zero waste pattern cutting is still pretty new.

Incidentally, there are plenty of boxy and voluminous fashions around which *aren't* zero waste (and could be).

Q: Can it be considered a zero waste sewing pattern if you require notions like bias tape or ribbing? What about contrast fabrics - should they be cut zero waste? Or should we only count the main fabric?

A: In my view: yes to the first two. I use bias binding a lot to finish edges, either as a facing or a binding. I count ribbing as a trim, and since such a small amount is needed for necks, wrists etc (and it comes in all sorts of widths) it's not possible to buy a certain amount for one garment and use it all. However, the pattern pieces for rib are almost always rectangular, leaving usable pieces for something else. I guess you could say the same thing about sewing thread, really.

Contrast fabrics should be cut zero waste too, since they're fabric, but typically much smaller amounts are needed. Try and cut contrasting pieces in a modular arrangement, so that the remainder of the fabric can be easily used for something else.

64

June

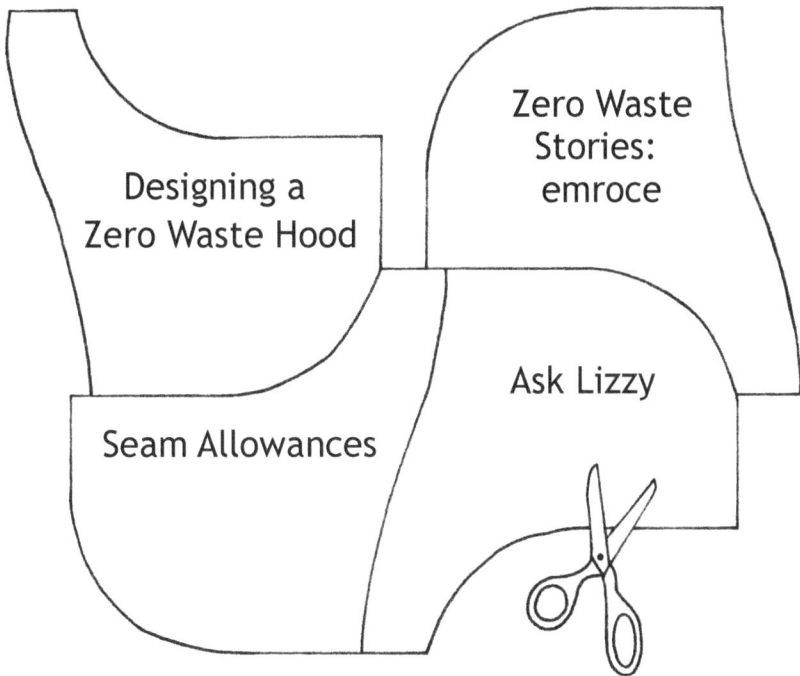

Designing a
Zero Waste Hood

Zero Waste
Stories:
emroce

Seam Allowances

Ask Lizzy

Designing a
Zero Waste Hood

A **hood** can be a very versatile neck finish. It can be used instead of, or with, a collar, and softens a neckline. I've used hoods on t-shirts when I couldn't get matching neck rib.

Unlike hats, which need to fit a particular head size, hoods are much easier-fitting. Typically, the neckline is the only part that needs grading, to fit onto different sized necks.

Some hoods are darted (usually at the shoulder) or pleated to fit the neckline, and either lap over or meet at the centre front. Hoodie hoods have a channel and drawcord on the front edge - note that cords aren't recommended for children's clothes.

The fabric's weight and drape is important and affects how the hood hangs on the head. A lining will give a hood structure and make it warmer.

Zero waste hoods can be made as **modular pattern pieces**, to be moved around the fabric wherever they fit best.

They can be made as **tessellating patterns**, which works well if you're cutting multiples for production.

Hoods can also be **nested into garment layouts**.

Here are some ideas for zero waste hoods. If you want to try making any of them, I've suggested some measurements which *include* **1cm/⅜" seam allowances and a 3cm/1¼" hem** around the face edge for a drawcord channel or hem. There's a patternmaking demonstration of these hoods on YouTube: https://www.youtube.com/watch?v=9idcpGTSY4o

66

Rectangular hood

This very basic hood, consisting of two rectangles, is the one I use most often for zero waste patterns. It could be cut as a single piece with a seam at the back only or at the top only. **1.** Cut two rectangles, 30.5cm/12" x 37.5cm/14¾". **2.** Sew two sides together as shown, and make a hem on one side. **3.** At the hood's peak, sew across to stop it looking too "pixie". Leave the excess fabric inside the hood or cut it off for something else. To fit the hood to the neckline, pleat or dart it if necessary.

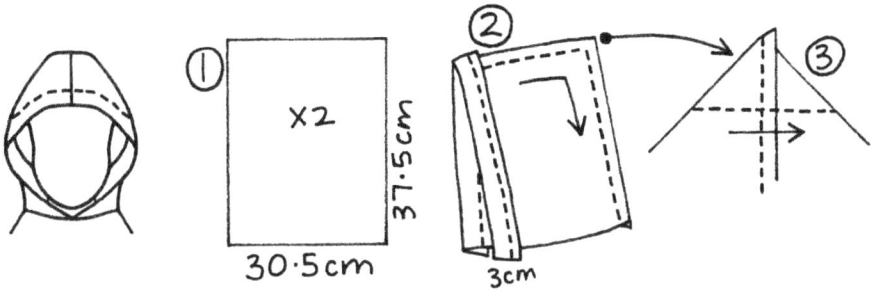

Tessellated hood

Many hoods curve around the neck, higher at the back and lower at the front. You can do this by tessellating the neck edge. **1.** Start with a rectangular hood and find the halfway point on the neck edge (point A). **2.** Measure up 2.5cm/1" and draw a curve. **3.** Cut this section off and pivot it on point A, and tape it to the other half of the neck. **4.** The necklines fit together neatly to form a rectangular unit.

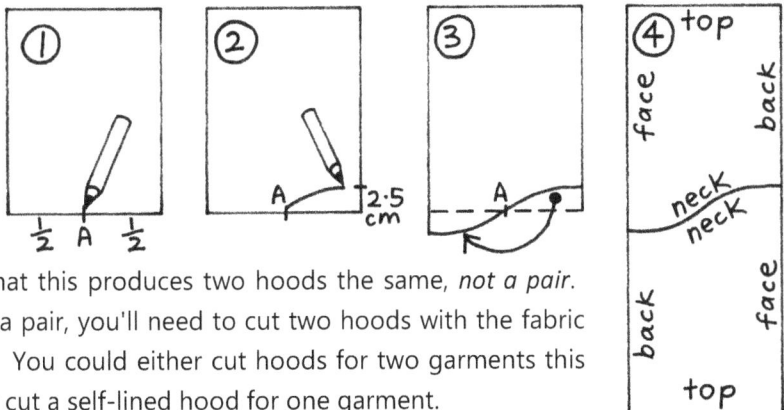

Note that this produces two hoods the same, *not a pair*. To get a pair, you'll need to cut two hoods with the fabric paired. You could either cut hoods for two garments this way, or cut a self-lined hood for one garment.

Using the neck cutout

Use the neck cutout as part of the hood, to make a bonnet-style hood. **1.** Front neck cutout, 19cm/7½" wide x 14cm/5½" deep **2.** Draw 3 sides of a shape: 22cm/8⅝" x 37.5cm/ 14¾" x 45.7cm/18". Connect the points for the fourth side. **3.** Find the centre of the diagonal side (point A). **4.** Draw a curve 2.5cm/1" deep. **5.** Cut off this shape and pivot it on point A, and tape it to the other half. **6.** Cut 2 of this shape, sew them together at the top of the head, and gather the curved edge to the neck cutout. Hem around the face edge.

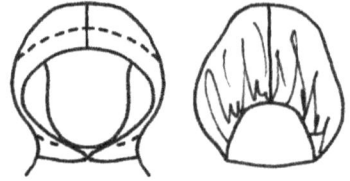

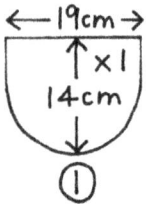

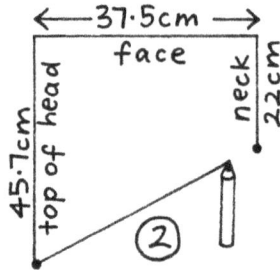

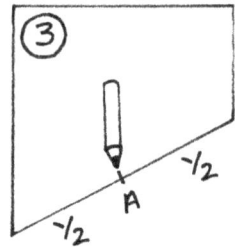

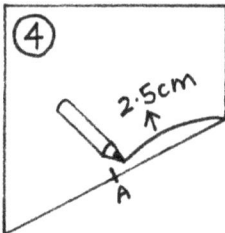

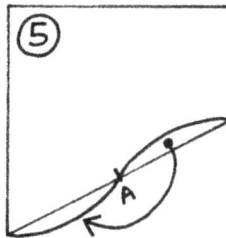

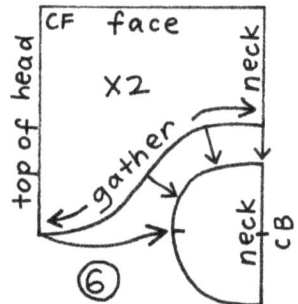

□ Cut the 2 hood pieces like this, but note that it produces two the same, *not a pair*. To get a pair, cut with paired fabric, which will give you a hood for two garments or a double-layered hood for one garment.

An oval-shaped neck cutout can be used for a hood's visor. 1. Neck cutout, 18.4cm/7¼" x 16.5cm/6½". **2.** Cut it in half horizontally, and sew the two pieces together on the curved edge (6mm/¼" seam). **3.** Turn through, press, and topstitch (in alternating directions) to give rigidity.

68

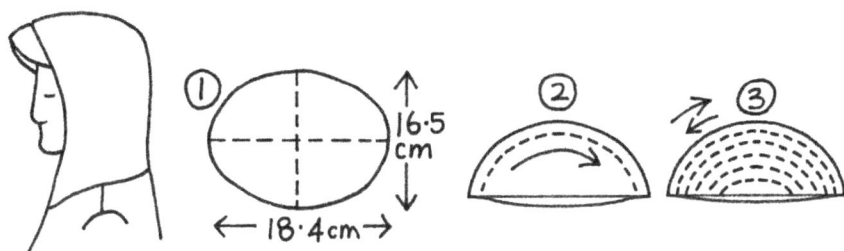

① ↕ 16·5 cm ← 18·4cm → ② ③

Mobius hood

Wear on its own or sew the back neck to a garment. The fabric has to look good on both sides. It *could* be handwoven on a narrow loom or knitted. Cut a rectangle 180cm/71" x 30.5cm/12".

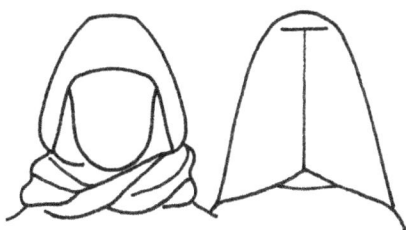

1. Sew the short sides together, twisting one first. 2. Stitch the back neck 26cm/10¼". Press open. Also, sew across the hood's peak (see page 67). 3. Hem the entire edge. 4. To wear, put your head in the hood part and loop the mobius around your neck.

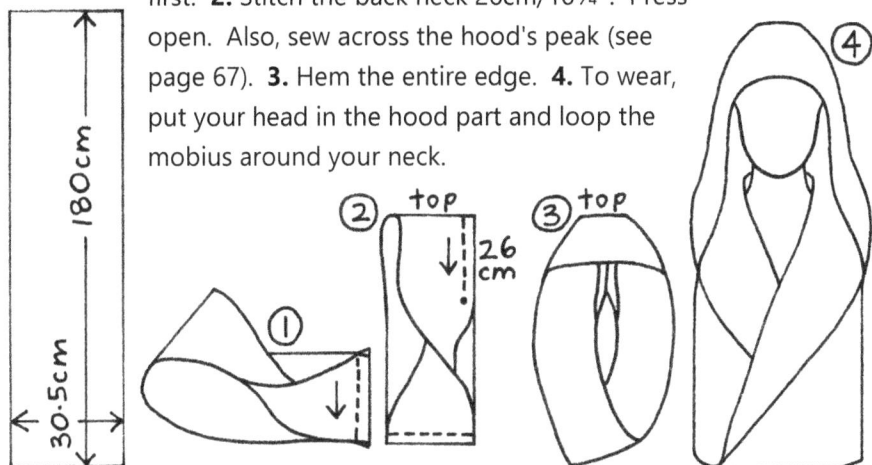

180cm

30·5cm

② top ↓ 26 cm ① ③ top ④

Adding ears to a hood

Tiny ears, made from the hood's curve, are sewn into a seam.
1. Take a rectangular hood and measure 13cm/5⅛" in from the front. Cut through and add a seam allowance to each edge. Also, measure 6.3cm/2½" in from the corner and draw a symmetrical curve. 2. To sew, lay the two curved cutoffs on

69

top of each other and cut in half. **3.** Sew the 2 short sides. **4.** Turn through and press. **5.** Sew the hood together, leaving the ear seam until last. Insert the ears about 7.5cm/3" down from the top.

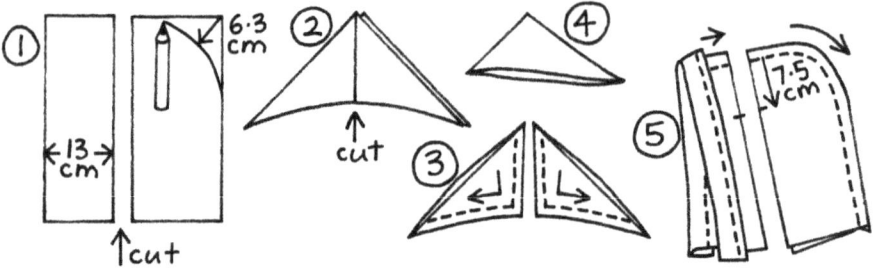

Hood cut from a square

A hood can be cut from a perfect square of fabric. The square's diagonal is the entire around-the-face measurement; use Pythagoras to calculate the square's sides. For example, 73.6cm/29" diagonal and 52cm/20½" sides **1.** Cut the square into 3 triangles as shown. **2.** Lay the two small triangles on the big one and sew the diagonal edges, pivoting at the corner. **3.** Open out and press the seams towards the small triangles. **4.** Fold the rectangle in half and sew the hood's back seam. Also, sew across the hood's peak, see page 67. Hem around the face. Note the top of the hood is a fold, the back is a seam, and the face and neck edges are on the bias.

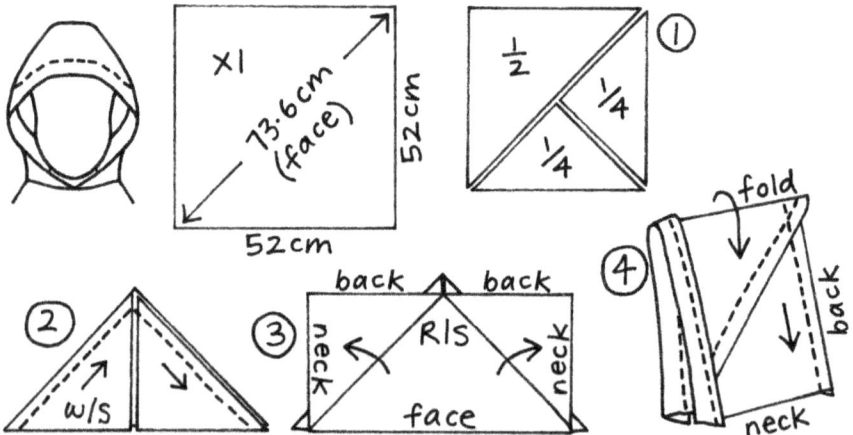

As the square is cut into triangles, you could also make it from triangles if you have any, say, from opposite corners of a larger square,

Hood with a gusset and extended fronts

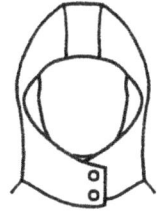

1. Begin with a rectangular hood and cut (2cm/¾") off the front hem, leaving just a seam allowance. **2.** Decide on a *finished* gusset width, from 7.5cm/3"-10cm/4". Cut **half** this amount off the back and discard. **3.** Draw the same amount on the top. **4.** Measure 4.5cm/1¾" in from the corner and draw a curve. **5.** Cut this whole section off and tape it to the front. **6.** Cut off the excess length (eg leave 10cm/4"). **7.** Tessellate the neck edge as described on page 67. Measure the *stitching* line around the hood to find the length needed for the gusset. Cut a rectangular gusset this length, and make the width the finished gusset width + two seam allowances.

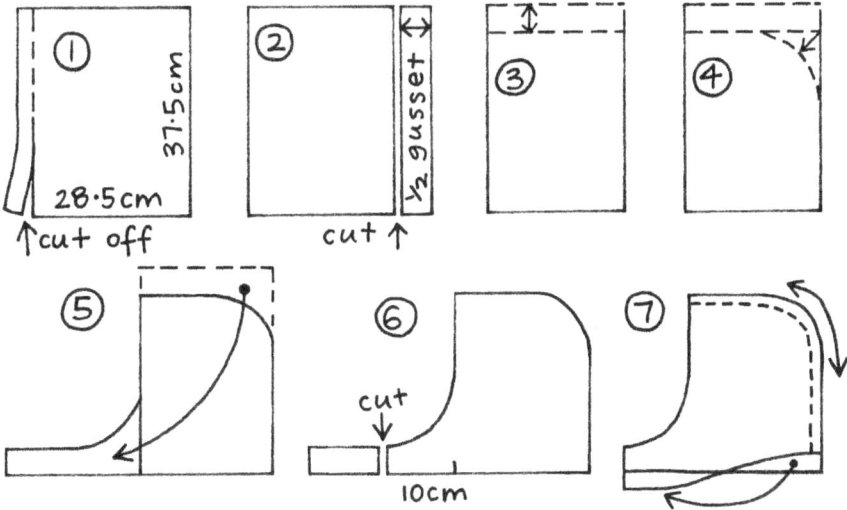

The pattern pieces tessellate like this, in pairs (L & R), with only a small amout of waste (shaded area) and some at the sides - the more hoods cut, the smaller % this will be. This idea is only suitable for cutting multiples of hoods.

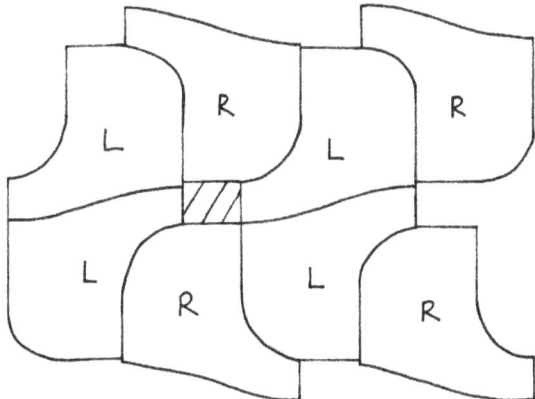

71

Seam Allowances
and
zero waste patterns

Seam allowances are one of the points of difference that zero waste patternmaking has from regular patternmaking.

- -
_____

Typically, computerized patternmaking invites you to add the seam allowances *after* you've made the pattern pieces, and the same approach is often used in manual patternmaking textbooks.

However, whether you make your patterns on computer or manually, with zero waste you'll need to work with **pieces that already have the seam allowance on them**.

If you're using a block/sloper/existing pattern piece as a guide, make sure it already has seam allowances added, otherwise you won't be able to interlock the pieces properly in the layout.
If you're an industry patternmaker, you may be used to doing this if you adapt patterns from a previous season's range to be used again.

When I make my patterns, I add the seam allowances as I go. For example, if I want a sleeve to *finish* at 26cm around the wrist, I'll draw it as 28cm so that I have a 1cm seam allowance each side. It eventually becomes a habit to work this way.
If you have complex shaped pieces with lots of curves, it may be trial-and-error to get the seam allowances right. If working on a computer, you might need to print out the pieces and check them manually by walking them around the curves.

Some seam allowance tips:

1. **Decide on the amount of seam allowance *before* you begin.**
The fabric will go some way towards helping you decide. For example, you might need wide seam allowances on thick fabric to help them lie flat. Or you might be using a knit fabric and it can be overlocked together, in which case 6mm/¼" is best.

2. **It's OK to use different seam allowances throughout.**
It's OK *as long as you make it very clear in the instructions*, because most home sewers aren't used to it, or expecting it.
A good example is reducing the need to trim back seams, such as around a neckline. For zero waste, you really want them pre-trimmed so you're not creating waste in the sewing process.

3. **Wider side seams help fine-tune fit.**
For example, 2cm/¾" side seams can help with making fitting adjustments on zero waste patterns; it makes the pattern more flexible size-wise. It's harder to do alterations on zero waste patterns, because the cutting layout IS the pattern - if you change one thing, the pieces around it will be affected. Bigger side seams allow the fit to be fine-tuned.

4. **Deeper hems give options for length.**
It may be impossible for a zero waste pattern to be made longer, but a deeper hem allowance will give more choices for the length. As with wider side seams, building in these options when you make the pattern will make it more inclusive and possibly give the garment greater longevity.

5. **Can you use the selvedge as part of the seam allowance?**
This is sometimes seen on vintage clothes, for centre back seams. The selvedge is included in an extra-wide seam allowance (up to 5cm/2") for the back of a skirt or coat. It gives the garment a bit more strength and substance, makes it alterable, can be harvested for mending, and makes use of the selvedges (provided they're not too rough to use).

emroce.

Inspiring the world to encourage ethical production & consumption.

Zero Waste Stories

emroce makes zero waste swimwear, designed to stay on in the surf. All pieces are made in Pāpāmoa, Aotearoa by founder, **Emma La Rocca**. Occasionally interns, neighbours & friends pop by to help with the simple sewing tasks, to pull through straps and to enhance the good vibes that keep the studio pumping out the most sustainable swimwear in New Zealand.

"I love being in my studio. It's too small and could be better organised but the instant I'm there, I'm calm. Along with the beach, the emroce studio is my happy place.

To make my swimwear, I use a high quality Italian fabric which is made with ECONYL® nylon. Acquafil SPA, the company behind this revolutionary fibre, supports The Healthy Seas Initiative, a group of 250 volunteer divers cleaning ghost fishing nets from our ocean floor. They melt these down, along with other nylon waste, to create ECONYL® nylon.

My discovery of ECONYL® back in 2011 was one of the deciding factors that got me into making swimwear. Before this, I exempted sportswear from needing to be sustainable as it's often made of plastic and at that time recycled fabrics hadn't come into the mainstream yet. I was teaching surfing in Chile while on my Overseas Experience and was sunbathing and reading a magazine between classes one day. There was an article in there about ECONYL® and I decided on the spot that I was going to make zero waste swimwear. I love being in the water and have never bought a bikini that I haven't had to alter to make it work better in the waves. I was introduced to

74

zero waste patternmaking back in 2008 by my 3rd year university teacher Holly McQuillan, co-author of *Zero Waste Fashion Design*, author of many articles on zero waste fashion, and cofounder of the Zero Waste Design Collective (ZWDC). I was already trying to cut my designs down to their simplest forms and was using only recycled or organic fabrics. So, to learn that I could also design with zero waste was a lightning bolt moment. It definitely made things more ecologically friendly, therefore had to be done.

After finishing university I dedicated my free time to practising my zero waste skills and finding my niche. The swimwear took a good year or two of trial and error to figure out. In the beginning I was cutting designs into too many different pieces. I was following the 'taught' design rules of making mood boards, designing funky things and trying to make them. It wasn't until I cut it back to simple shapes and allowed my zero waste pattern making process to inspire the styles, that I finally pumped out my first collection. In 2016, after two years of trialing, the first collection suddenly took two weeks to finalize.

Having a zero waste business has so many benefits. Using zero waste patterns alongside eco friendly fabrics puts us a step ahead in the game of sustainable fashion. It saves so much money which has been a huge help in growing emroce. With normal patternmaking an average of 30% of fabric is thrown away, so for every 10 rolls of fabric bought, 3 are biffed straight into landfill. It's a huge waste especially when we're looking at fast fashion.

My main goal is to encourage larger fashion companies to use zero waste pattern making techniques. I see emroce as a laboratory for testing zero waste pattern methods and business models which can be used in fast fashion companies. Thanks to ZWDC this goal has started to become a reality. Early in 2022 alongside a handful of other zero waste pattern makers (including Liz Haywood), I was called in to work on a project with Decathlon, the world's largest sporting goods retailer. Decathlon is the first huge fashion house to be convinced of the benefits of working with zero waste patterns. In their first year of applying zero waste pattern practices to their designs, they saved a whopping 783km of 140cm width fabric from going to landfill. That's almost the length of the North Island of New Zealand, Te Ika A Maui. We hope that other fashion companies will now follow suit."

www.emroce.com   @emroceswimwear

75

Ask Lizzy

Q: **What if the fabric width required for a zero waste pattern doesn't match my fabric's width?**

A: If it's too narrow, you could piece a strip on one or both sides. You could also sew together several pieces of fabric to create the yardage you need. This can work very well for bias cut garments; the lines sewn on the straight grain accentuate the bias cut.

If it's too wide, cut the excess off the side - you'll have a handy rectangular piece for something else. You might be able to use it on the garment for a belt, frill, etc.

For both, you might be able to turn the layout around 90 degrees and cut it out that way - it depends on the fabric type, width & length, and the size you're making whether you're able to do this.

Sometimes a small variation in fabric width doesn't matter - your garment will just be a little longer/shorter/have a deeper hem/more ease/etc.

Q: **How did you transition from being a regular patternmaker to making *only* zero waste patterns?**

A: At the beginning of 2020, I decided I was *only* going to make zero waste patterns from now on. I reached a tipping point where I just didn't see a way forward with regular patterns anymore. However, it was fairly easy to do because I wasn't working as a patternmaker immediately before that. I'd moved to the country, had children, was promoting *The Dressmaker's Companion*, teaching pop-up sewing classes, and about to launch *Zero Waste Sewing*.

It would be much harder for someone currently working as a patternmaker or freelancing for people not interested in zero waste. In that situation, your transition to solely zero waste patterns might be more gradual.

July

Zero Waste Historical Clothes	Make a Eura Dress	
Zero Waste Stories: Process of Sewing	Ask Lizzy	

Zero Waste
Historical Clothes

As I'm sure you already know, modern zero waste patterncutting has its roots in weaving and loom widths from long ago. Which is why looking at historical clothing is an essential and helpful starting point for designing modern zero waste clothes.

Historical cutting layouts, designed to fit perfectly within the fabric's width, typically have **all the cut lines as straight as possible**, with few, if any, curves. Some are made up entirely of squares and rectangles. In many layouts, the width of the fabric is the width of the garment's body.

The selvedges are cleverly used to save the sewing of hems/neatening of edges and give strength where needed.

To create fullness, fabric is cut diagonally and the pieces reversed so there's flare at the hemline. Sometimes *extra* lengths of fabric are cut diagonally and added to the sides to make them wider at the hem.

The fabric is pieced cleverly in unnoticeable places, such as under the arm. Often **gussets** are used for shape and to add strength, and **extra layers of fabric** are added to strategic areas to make the garment sturdier and last longer.

Zero waste historical clothes loosely fall into 3 types:

Traditional clothes which are still worn every day, on special occasions, or for a particular trade/profession. These are living examples of historic zero waste patterncutting. The best source is primary - maybe you live in a country with a rich textile tradition, have a friend who does, or you've visited.

Otherwise, look in books such as *Cut my Cote* or ones with titles such as *Traditional Clothes of (insert country here)*. Online searches are easier if you have the correct name for a particular item of clothing.

While you do need to be careful about cultural appropriation, there's a lot you can learn from examining cutting layouts and sewing methods.

Ancestors of the clothes we wear now. Often there's a direct, traceable lineage. Men's shirts are an excellent example. Their predecessor is no longer worn, but a gradual transformation to the modern shirt is easy to trace.

Clothes unearthed by archeologists. Sometimes there are only mere fragments of cloth remaining. Archeologists make educated guesses at the cut, style and details, based on the evidence available, knowledge of the era, and practical cutting and sewing.

How to use an historic zero waste cutting layout

Typically, these are presented as more of an idea than an actual pattern - it's usually a drawing of a cutting layout with no or few measurements, and no sewing instructions. This can be pretty daunting, and maybe you have been put off by the lack of detail.

1. Study the diagram and establish what's what (eg neckline, waist, underarm etc) so you understand the layout. Make a paper model if necessary. Actually, a paper model is a really good idea - it will help you think about the sewing order and how the pieces relate to one another.

2. Plug in some measurements, which *include ease and seam allowances*. Either: measure and compare a similar fitting garment you have, measure yourself and add ease, or use a basic block as a guide. Determine the length too. Don't rush this bit! This will become your cutting guide.

3. Cut and sew a sample, taking notes so that you can replicate it or make changes. Is there a formula for this layout? Or a crucial measurement on which everything hinges (eg a waist measurement)? Understanding this will be the key to making multiples sizes.

Making a Eura Dress

The **Eura dress** falls into the "archeology" category of historical zero waste clothes.

Eura, in south-western Finland, is an area long-famous for archeological remains found in burial sites, with remains dating from 500AD-1200AD. The Luistari cemetery is the largest Iron Age burial ground in Finland, with over 1,300 graves found, but textile evidence is rare due to the fabric rotting away in the soil. No complete garments survive, so the cut and construction is built on speculation based on small fragments of textiles.

The Eura dress was reconstructed from evidence found in a single grave from the early 11th century. The woman's grave contained jewelry and ornamented clothes, and the metallic oxides released by the metals had preserved fragments of textiles. Although there were no large pieces of fabric, there were enough pieces at strategic points to attempt to reconstruct her costume.

It was believed she was wearing a dark blue woollen underdress with long sleeves that were narrow at the wrists, widening at the top, with the fabric's warp parallel to the length. In keeping with known clothes from other Iron Age finds in Northern Europe, it was supposed the dress was cut with low or zero waste.

Several trials were made of possible patterns based on shirt-like tunics...

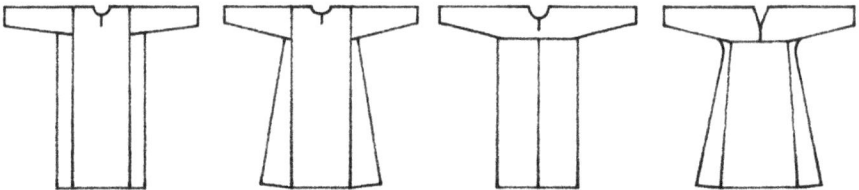

...before finding a probable pattern gleaned from a leather tunic found in a Danish bog of assumed Iron Age date.

Yes, it's entirely possible it didn't look like this, but it didn't conflict with the evidence of the grave and known features of clothes at the time.

The Eura dress is zero waste, cut from a single rectangle. It has long sleeves, a V-neck, a flared skirt and side gussets which extend from the sides to under the arms.

There are no closures; it pulls on over the head. The front and back are the same.

Suitable fabrics include light to medium weight wovens. Consider cutting up a flannelette sheet to make a winter nightie.

How much fabric? The original dress used a piece 160cm wide x 190cm long, but of course the dimensions can be changed.

The fabric *length* depends on how long you want the dress. Try 190cm for long, 175cm for three-quarter or 160cm for knee length.

To find the fabric *width,* take your bust measurement and multiply it by 1.23 to give you a *mimimum* width. This will give you a dress with about 10cm/4" ease, so feel free to round this up for a looser-fitting dress.

Note that this is just a guide; Eura is a tricky pattern to predict the finished

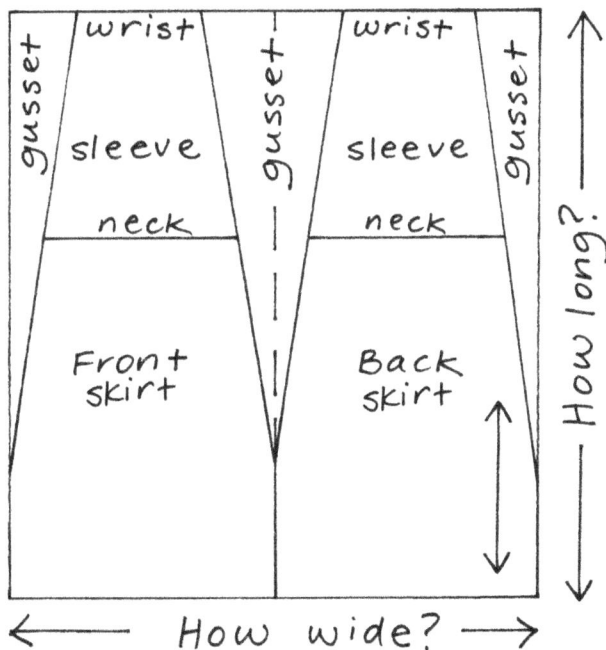

size, because the angles of the gusset/sleeve/skirt change as the measurements change.

Also note that unfortunately there's no way to add bust shaping, so the hemline will rise at the front with large busts.

If you're cutting to a particular fabric width:

115cm/45" wide will make a dress measuring about 104cm/41" around the chest. The armhole depth will be about 21.5cm/8.5".

150cm/59" wide fabric will make a dress measuring about 127cm/50" around the chest, with an armhole depth of about 28cm/11".

The selvedges can run either way. The original layout has them at the sides, so the gusset seams are conveniently neatened for you. If you have the selvedges at the top and bottom (eg if you're using a sheet), you won't need to hem the sleeves and skirt.

This YouTube video shows some cutting and construction demonstrations:
https://www.youtube.com/watch?v=5yI720VIMAY

For large sizes and/or narrow fabric widths, cut it in two pieces like this. Therefore, you'll need *double* the length and *half* the width suggested above.

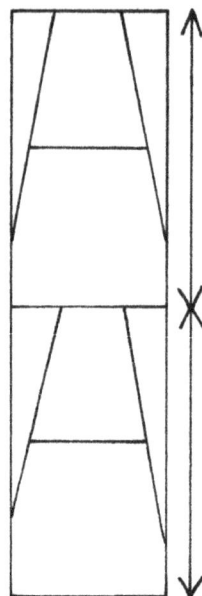

To cut

1. Fold the fabric in half or lay the two pieces together.

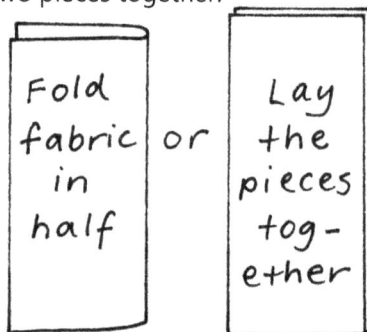

Fold fabric in half or Lay the pieces tog-ether

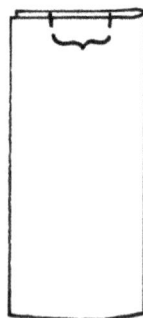

2. Mark in the wrist width, centred at the top of the fabric. Try 28cm/11" - 33cm/13" *or* measure loosely around your wrist and add two 1cm/⅜" seam allowances.

82

3. Measure up 25cm/10" from the bottom corners. (Why? It stops the gussets from being *too* pointy at the ends.)

4. Connect the points to draw the triangular gussets.

5. Measure down from the top for the sleeve length. 79cm/31" works for "average" length arms
or
measure yourself from centre to wrist and add 7.5cm/3"-10cm/4" for two hems (neck and wrist) and ease.

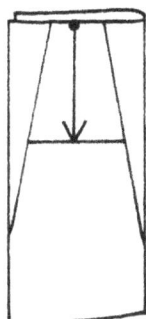

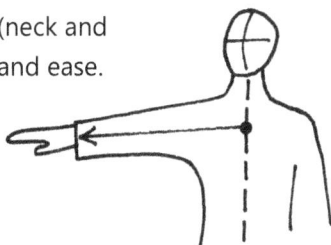

6. Cut out. Sew the 2-part gusset together with a 6mm/¼" seam. Sometimes the other gusset has a false seam so they match.

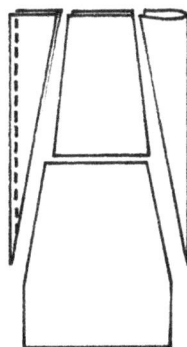

I can attest that you won't notice any difference either way when you're wearing the dress.

To sew

Take 1cm/⅜" seam allowances and 2.5cm/1" hems.

Here's an overview of how the pieces go together:

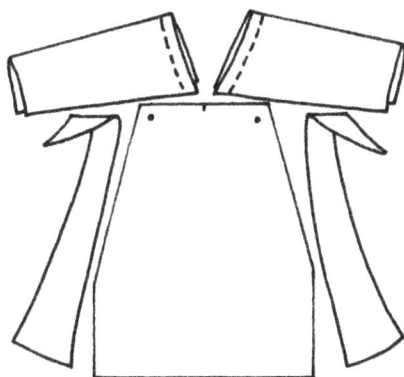

The wide ends of the sleeve form the neckline.

1. Hem the necklines 2.5cm/1", by hand or machine.

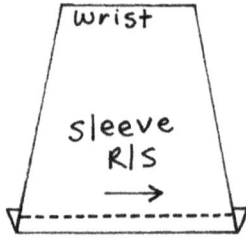
wrist

sleeve
R|S
→

Make sure you hem the correct edge! (It's the *wide* end of the sleeve.) If you're adding a label, sew it to the hem allowance before stitching, or slip a label under the edge.

2. Arrange the two sleeves like this:

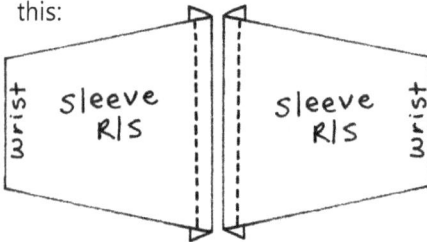
wrist — sleeve R|S — sleeve R|S — wrist

The necklines can meet in the centre *or* overlap by the width of the hem but no more than this or it won't sit flat.

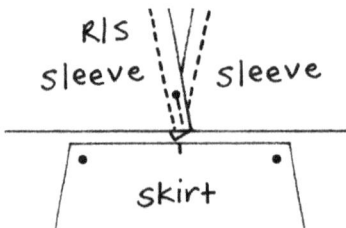
R|S
sleeve — sleeve
skirt

Attach the sleeves to the skirt, stopping 1cm/⅜" short of each end of the front/back. Overlock and press towards the skirt.

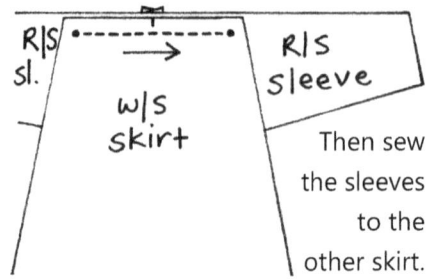
R|S sl. — w|s skirt — R|S sleeve

Then sew the sleeves to the other skirt.

3. Sew the gussets to the sides, starting at the bottom of the skirt. Sew with the skirt uppermost. The skirt's raw edge will have a slight obtuse angle (from Steps 3 & 4, cutting) but just smooth this off as you sew. Stop and start the seam at the skirt/sleeve junction. There may be overhanging gusset at the wrist (cut this off) or it may stop short of the end. Press and overlock.

Are you adding pockets? See page 85. Sew them in at the same time.

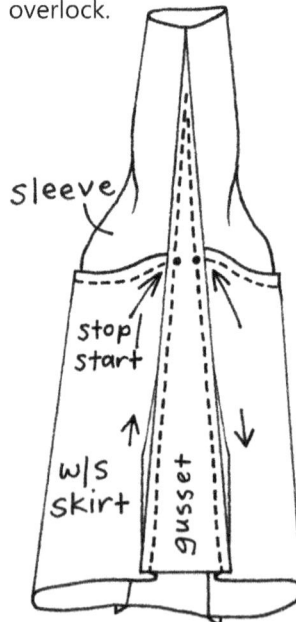
sleeve — stop start — w|s skirt — gusset

84

4. Try the dress on. At the back neck, stitch it up a little way if it looks better. You could also add button/s to the front.

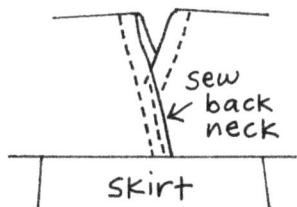

Hem the sleeves and skirt.

Adding a hood and/or in-seam pockets

For both together you need 37cm/14½" of 115cm/45" wide fabric. Fold it in half and mark in the hood next to the selvedges.

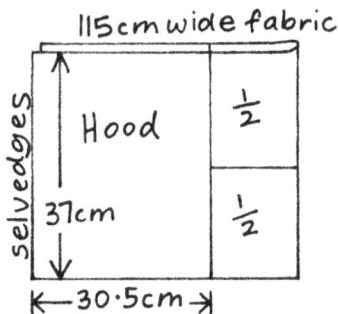

Divide the remaining piece into two. Open these out and lay them together, right sides of the fabric facing each other. Measure 20cm/8" along each side and connect the points.

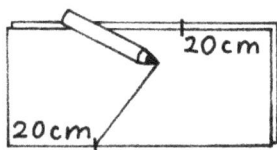

For no hood, just pockets, use the pocket pattern on page 8.

Sew the **hood** as shown below and neaten the lower edge. On the dress, stitch the back neck up, then sit the hood inside the neckline and sew the hood to the edge.

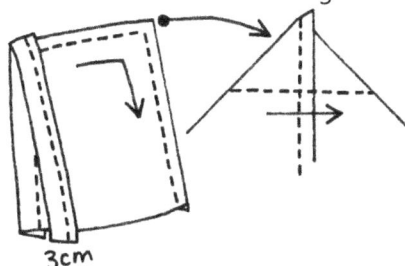

On the **pockets**, mark in a 15cm/6" hand opening, 2.5cm/1" down from the top.

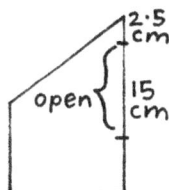

Mark a matching opening in the gusset/skirt seam.

1. For all 4 pocket pieces: align a pocket piece on the dress and sew a 6mm/¼" seam. Overlock. Press towards the pocket.

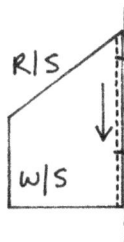

2. Lay the pocket bags together and sew around the edges. Sew the gusset/skirt seam leaving a gap for the hand opening. Overlock around the pocket.

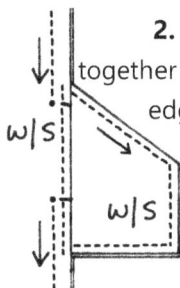

85

Process of Sewing
By Maureen Gleason

Maureen Gleason is the designer behind **Process of Sewing**, developing zero waste sewing patterns for the home sewer. She is a theatre maker and textile artist based in Berlin, Germany, but was born and raised in rural Minnesota, USA.

Maureen studied in an acting conservatory with the Guthrie BFA actor training program in Minneapolis, MN before earning her MFA with Rose Bruford College, London in Embodied Dramaturgy. During her BFA, Maureen was introduced to costume design. She currently develops the costumes for her theatre collective, *Hopefully, Maybe*.

Her grandmother is her hometown's unofficial tailor and is the true inspiration behind Maureen's desire to explore the field of textiles. She grew up watching her grandmother create useful items from seemingly nothing; hand towels, clothing, blankets and toys were constantly emerging from her magical hands.

What sticks with Maureen, however, and is most likely the reason for her interest in zero waste drafting methods, is her grandmother's undeniable thriftiness. What Maureen's generation would call sustainable, her grandmother would simply call practical. Her grandmother's sewing closet is full of every leftover scrap, zipper and thread cutting - even plastic bread bags - and all of it seems to find its way seamlessly back into her work.

"Process of Sewing has been the perfect outlet for my inner artist and designer to meet. These two elements of myself are not often felt at the same time, but by challenging them both to

Zero Waste Stories

86

sit down and listen to each other, week after week, they are slowly learning how to better express themselves as a team. The artistic element of Process of Sewing for me is the never ending quest to answer the question *Why and how do we get dressed?*

Sewing is a way to meet new shades of myself through the act of clothing different aspects of my psyche. As I continue to develop the skill and grow my wardrobe, I am shocked to see just how linked it is to what I would think is my "private" life: each color choice or fabric choice revealing to the world my most personal feelings and desires. With each make I grow braver, and I'm sure far off into the future I'll have an entirely "revealing" wardrobe to show for it.

As my artistic voice gets stronger, I have also found myself merging my zero waste practices into non-functional pieces of textile art as well. I hope to share more reflections and insights regarding my artistic journey at some point in the future.

As for my inner designer, discovering zero waste drafting has been a breakthrough for me creatively. Zero waste drafting is the perfect method for anyone who experiences creative overload. It can be easy to get overwhelmed by the sheer possibility of what "could be made" instead of actually sitting down to simply "make". Coming back to a structure is what keeps me out of my head and into the piece. With zero waste drafting, there is a logic that has to be followed in order for the piece to be realized, and it is this limitation that gives me inspiration and flow.

Zero waste pattern drafting is also a great way to fine tune your listening skills. When you make a piece of theatre, it is always a dialogue. With zero waste drafting it's the same way. It's a back and forth process that has you continually asking, *if I change this, how does it shift the rest of the pieces, and how will it affect my piece of fabric as a whole?* The important thing for me has been to learn to really listen to the answer, and change my vision for the final outcome as the fabric tells me what it needs."

@processofsewing   https://processofsewing.etsy.com

Ask Lizzy

Q: **Why don't we just use scrap fabric for stuffing?**

A: There are multiple ways of doing zero waste, and many home sewers do just that - save their scraps for stuffing. Some prolific sewers have found, though, that there's a limit to the number of cushions, poufs, bolsters and soft toys that their homes can hold!

Why don't we collect textile waste from factories? It could be sorted by the cutting department into fibre types and, unlike second hand clothes, factory waste is unworn, clean-ish and doesn't have haberdashery attached. Yes, this is being done and some textile waste is shredded to make stuffing, if it can't be used in other ways. Note that there's an intermediate step, which is shredding the fabric - it can't be used as-is because it would be too lumpy and heavy.

You could argue that it's better to turn it into stuffing rather than throw it into landfill, and yes, of course it is.

However, we can do better by not making the scraps in the first place, and you knew I was going to say that, didn't you? But doesn't the current system sound like madness? We're recycling virgin fabric for stuffing - fabric that's new and hasn't been used at all for its intended purpose. We should be using lesser quality materials for stuffing, not making new fabric and then immediately recycling it into a lower grade material.

Q: **Are there any fabrics that make it difficult to do zero waste?**

A: I think there are. If the fabric is napped (velvet, corduroy, faux fur etc) or has a directional print, then the pattern pieces can't be topped-and-tailed within the layout; they all have to run in the same direction, which limits what you can do with them. If I could name a fabric that's *easiest* for zero waste, it's boiled wool. It's non-fray, pliable, easy to cut and sew, presses well, can be cut in any direction and it's the same on both sides.

August

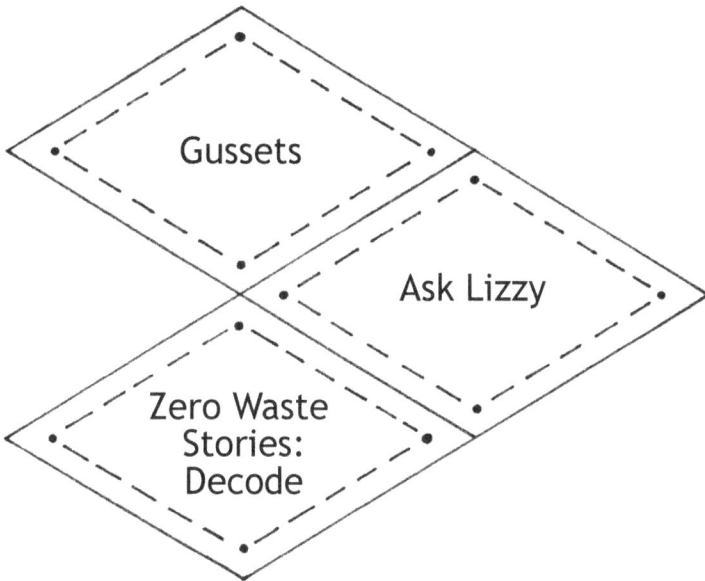

Gussets

Ask Lizzy

Zero Waste
Stories:
Decode

Gussets
and how to use them

Gussets are a very Old School, nay historical, way of giving **shape and movement** to clothes. A gusset will give movement where you want it without making the garment too big, making relatively slim-fitting clothes possible.

Underarm gussets were used frequently in the 1950s, for tops and coats with magyar sleeves. This was probably the last great era for gussets; in my view, they're underutilized in fashion today.

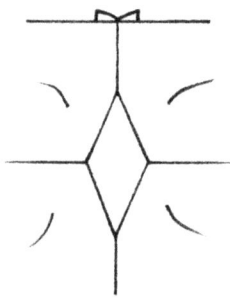

As well as shape and movement, gussets **add strength** by redistributing stress points on a seam. Instead of four seams coming together at a single point, for instance, the stress is shifted across the gusset. The gusset acts as strain relief and also adds a bit of extra room. Therefore, gussets can potentially make garments last longer, because the cloth isn't damaged due to strain.

As a bonus, a gusset **reduces bulk** from having all the seam allowances meeting in one spot.

Gussets can also be used to **make an area adjustable**, just like the tongue on a sneaker. For example, the back of men's trousers in the 18th-19th century used a gusset and ties to tighten them. Sometimes a buckle and tab was used.

back waist

90

Maternity trousers (or indeed, any trousers if you want an adjustable waist) can have a front adjustable closure with a gusset and lacing.

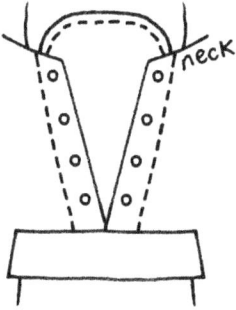
front waist

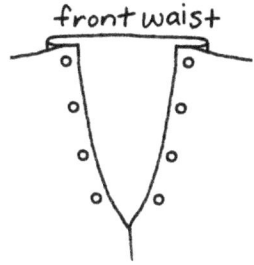
neck

The same idea is repeated on the front neck of fisherman's smocks.

Again, on the back of waistcoats.

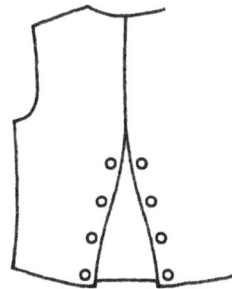

Gussets are **advantageous for zero waste**. They allow you to put shaping in areas while keeping the other pattern pieces more rectangularly shaped (and therefore easier to fit together). With shapes like trousers, for example, a crotch gusset will let you fit the main pieces closer together and cut the gusset elsewhere, which will save fabric.

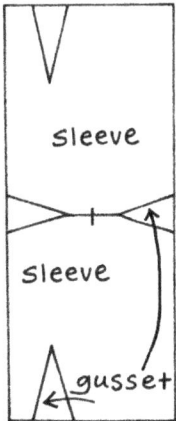
sleeve

sleeve

gusset

Since gussets are fairly small pieces, on a zero waste layout they can be cut from small areas in between the bigger pieces. This example has triangular gussets fitted around sleeves.

Alternatively, if you're designing for production and cutting multiple garments at once, the gussets could be tessellated and cut together. Triangles and diamonds naturally fit together.

This leaves you with half shapes at each end, though.

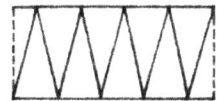

cut
waist
gusset
hem

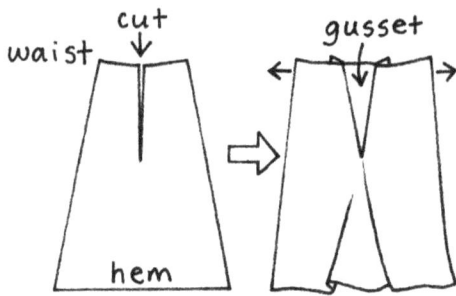

Gussets can **create fullness in other areas of the garment**. Madeleine Vionnet used triangular gussets at the waist, inserted into slashes. When the slashed part is spread to receive the gusset, the hemline slackens into ripples.

How to make a pattern for a gusset

Gussets are used at underarms, trouser crotches, neck/shoulders, and for bust or hip flare. The shape is usually triangular or diamond, but can also be eye-shaped or square/rectangular. Making the pattern pieces can involve some trial-and-error.

But first, a quick sewing tutorial...

Gussets can be sewn into a *seam* or a *slash*. A slash is not as robust as a seam, so care needs to be taken with sewing and fabric choice - firmly woven fabrics which don't fray much work best. It's a bit more challenging sewing-wise, too.

To sew a gusset in a seam

✂ Sew the gusset part *first*, then sew the remainder of the seam. Be sure to stitch the gusset *only on the seam line*, not from raw-edge-to-raw-edge — put a dot in the corners of the gusset at the seam junctions if it helps. The corners of the gusset should always be loose; if they aren't, the gusset won't sit flat. The exception is when a garment is being overlocked together with 6mm/¼" seam allowances eg for stretch knit fabrics.

✂ After sewing, press the seams *away* from the gusset and topstitch (on the garment side) for strength.

✂ The seam allowance can be any amount, but the gusset needs to have the same.

To sew a gusset in a slash, the slash needs to be stabilized first. **1.** Mark the slash line on the right side of the fabric. **2.** On the wrong side, thoroughly fuse a circle of interfacing over the point. Some people fuse the entire slash. **3.** Using a short stitch length, stay-stitch to the point, stitch across the point with one stitch, then sew the other side. Sew ON the stitching line. **4.** Cut *exactly* to the point. **5.** Put the gusset and garment right sides together, and match the slash's point and the gusset's point with a pin, slash uppermost. Still with a tiny stitch length, sew to the point. **6.** Pivot with the needle down, move the fabric around the needle and sew the second side of the slash to the gusset. Carefully overlock. **7.** Press the seam away from the gusset and topstitch around the gusset to make it stronger.

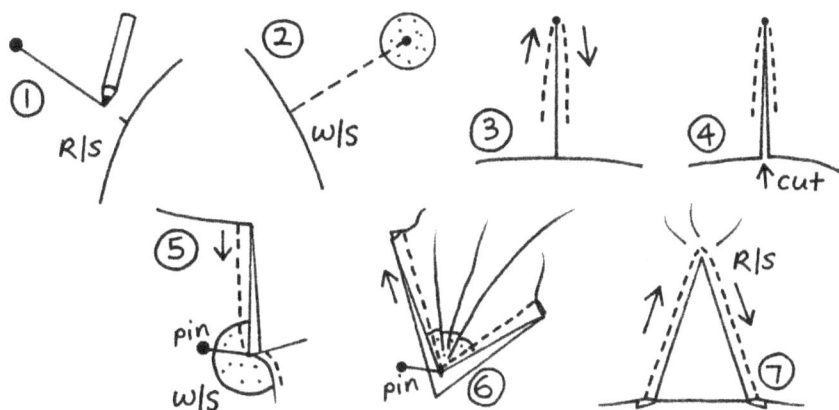

✂ A slash is easier to sew if it's rounded or teardrop shaped instead of a point. This gives a sturdier apex, since the strain is spread, but obviously it looks a bit different. Fuse and stay-stitch the rounded apex, snip multiple times to the stitching, then spread the slash apex to sew the gusset in.

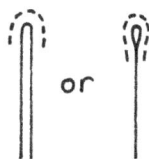

Underarm gussets can be inserted into a seam or a slash.

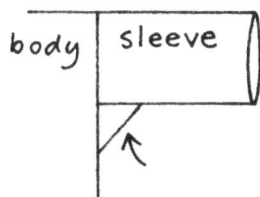

A simple square gusset is oft-seen on historical shirts, chemises and similar T-shaped garments such as crocheted granny square coats.

The gusset is cut as a square, but when sewn in place it forms a triangle, with the bias of the square conveniently running in the direction of reaching up or out - right where the stretch is needed.
10cm/4" square is a good size to cut (with 1cm/⅜" seams included). You could go to 11.5cm/4½" but too much bigger will give a batwing effect.

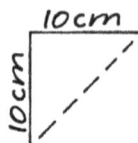

To sew. 1. Stitch the gusset on one side of the sleeve, finishing 1cm/⅜" from the end. Overlock just that little seam. **2.** Sew the adjacent side to the other underarm of the sleeve (A), and then carry on to sew the sleeve's underarm seam. Overlock. **3.** If you're inserting the sleeve into a slit rather than an armhole seam, sew the gusset *before* cutting the slit so you can measure the sleeve to get the exact length.

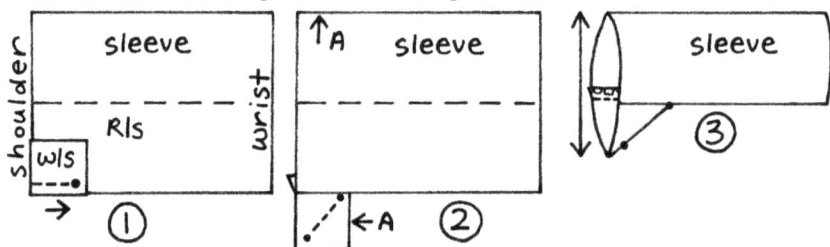

Gussets inserted into an **underarm slash** are typically diamond shaped. Draw a pattern for the diamond, with the length of the stitching lines corresponding to the slash. A possible size might be 10cm/4" by 7cm/¾".
Sometimes the pattern is made in two parts, with the underarm seam through the middle of the gusset. However, a diamond is less bulky than two triangles.

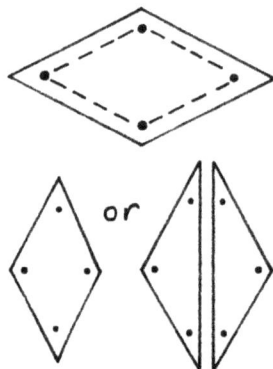

✂ Underarm gussets can rescue a too tight underarm/bicep, and can be retro-fitted with only a small amount of unpicking.
✂ Underarm gussets can also be long diamonds or long eye-shapes, extending to the elbow and waist. They can also be designed as a long rectangular strip, extending from hemline to wrist.

Trouser gussets are usually triangles or diamonds, and are inserted into seams rather than slashes.

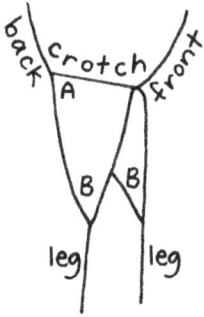

Triangular gussets sit folded in half inside the trousers, with the straight side at the front and the points extending down each leg.

The garment's front and back are usually straight, with a notch for the gusset.

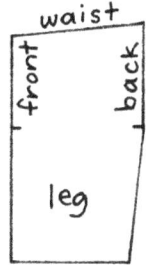

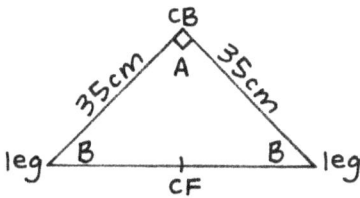

These work best in looser-fitting trousers, because there's a weak point at the front. The triangle is a right angle triangle, and a typical size might be 35cm/13¾" on the two shorter sides.

Diamond or eye-shaped gussets are seen on jeans made specifically for motor bike riders. Action star Chuck Norris wore them too, for kicking his opponents in the face! They're also used for horseriding trousers and leggings. The advantage, apart from movement, is the wearer isn't sitting on a bulky 4-seam junction.

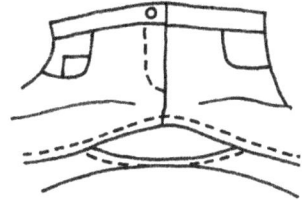

Make a pattern. 1. Put the crotch extensions of the trousers together, lapping the seam allowances, and draw in where you'd like the gusset seams. **2.** Cut off the triangle and use it to draw a diamond gusset shape, taking care of whatever seam allowances you have on the pattern. **3.** Often the diamond's obtuse angles are rounded off to make sewing easier and give a smoother seam line.

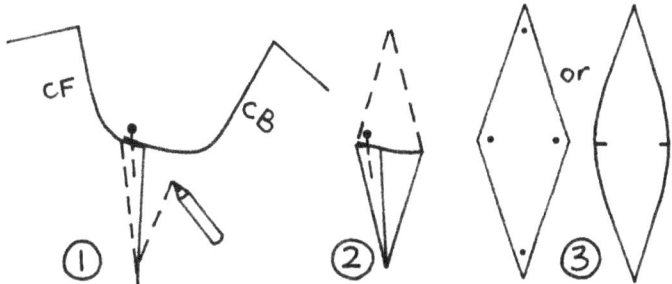

If you're putting a gusset in **shorts** (eg short leg swimsuits or undies), the ends of the gusset will form part of the hemline.

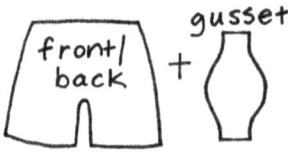

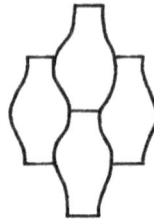

The gusset can be tessellated if you're cutting multiples.

Shoulder/neck gussets are always triangular and are inserted into a seam or slash. The width of the gusset contributes to the circumference of the neckline.

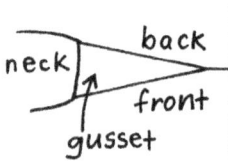

They're rarely seen on modern clothes, because they can be replaced by simply sloping the shoulder.

Historically, **neck gussets** were added to men's square cut shirts to relieve strain at the neck/shoulder point. These gussets weren't very big - they didn't extend the full length of the shoulder.

The gussets were cut as squares about 8cm/3" (two squares per shirt) and then cut in half diagonally to make triangles.

One triangle was sewn by hand into a slash made for the neck, then another triangle was sewn underneath so that all the seam allowances were enclosed. The bias side of the gusset then became part of the neckline, which was gathered to the collar. For extra strength, a strip of fabric was appliquéd the length of the shoulder (on the wrong side), including the gusset.

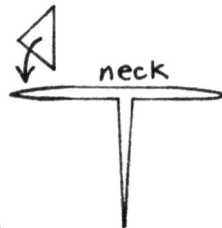

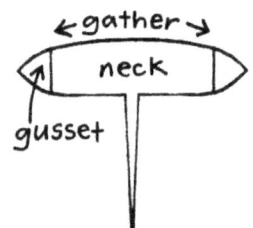

However, this type of gusset is too small to give a smooth shoulder line - the gusset really needs to extend the full length of the shoulder. It's also much easier to sew by machine into a *seam* rather than a *slash*.

Since a typical shoulder is about 4cm/1½" higher at the neck than the shoulder, and about 12cm-13cm/5" long, a triangular shaped gusset could be about 8cm/3" at the neck and 12cm-13cm/5" long, finished size.

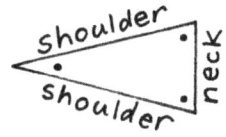

Bust and hip gussets are triangular and inserted into a seam or a slash. They're seen on jackets, corsets and corset-style evening dresses.

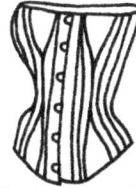

They work like a reverse dart - instead of stitching fabric together at the narrowest point (ie the waist), the gusset spreads the fabric at the widest points (the bust and/or hips). Handily, the size of the gusset can be changed without changing the size of the garment.

Two questions about gussets

1. Do gussets get graded? Some do and some don't. It's helpful to remember how the garment grows in that area - the same will apply for the gusset. Some gussets get deeper but not wider, or vice versa.

2. What's the difference between a gusset, gore and godet?

A *gusset* is always functional and often in a discrete place.

A *gore* is a panel added to the entire length of the garment, wider at one end. For example, a 6-gore skirt.

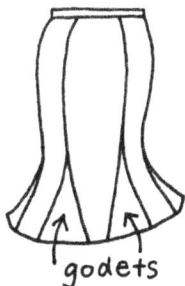

A *godet* is the gusset's glamorous, showy, cousin. It's a triangular shape used to add flare. Like a gusset, it's inserted into a seam or slash.

DECODE

Danielle Elsener of DECODE has dedicated her life's work to proving zero waste as a valid and robust design model. For over a decade, she's learned from industry, educational institutions, and self-run initiatives to understand how best to do this.

"We are the world's first Zero Waste Apparel Manufacturing Facility! We are a factory built with the premise of only manufacturing zero waste garments. We run our own inhouse label (DECODESUPPLY.COM), offer wholesale manufacturing (blank tees, etc) and some white label manufacturing. We also are very much in the world of education and sharing our experiences with the next generation. Most of our sewers are right out of college and are receiving a crash course in zero waste design along with their industrial sewing training. It's really exciting to be giving this kind of knowledge to those who are going to change the industry of the future!

I began sewing when I was 10 years old, when my parents gave me a sewing lesson for Christmas. My high school had a great arts program and I began learning about the fashion world from a young age. This allowed me to understand what I wanted to do early on and set me up for going to SCAD for my undergrad.

Like a lot of zero waste designers, I discovered the work of Holly McQuillan and Timo Rissanen, Julien Roberts, and Rickard Lindqvist. Their approaches to creative pattern cutting and system design shook my design world and my entire method of making was completely changed. I could no longer go back to a more traditional method of design - there seemed to be no

Zero Waste Stories

98

point in that. I love giving reason to everything I do, and developing a system to design into felt like the natural course of my design journey.

At DECODE MFG, education is a huge part of our business. Most of the pieces I currently make are meant to not "look" zero waste. This is to help dispel the notion that all zero waste clothing is oversized, boxy or eco-chic. I started with the hardest thing of all - the basics: tees, hoodies, sweatpants, etc. If someone looks at our ZW tee, they wouldn't know right off the bat that it's zero waste. This can then lead to a customer not understanding our brand vision or price point. There's a disconnection between the pieces and the story if you don't take the time to get into the "why" behind it.

Not only do we need to talk about zero waste design, but we need to educate how greenwashed the industry is, and why the customer should care about having a tee that was made in Brooklyn, out of fabric made in the USA, by sewers who make well above living wage, and most of all, zero waste. Try doing all of that in a sentence or two!

I opened DECODE MFG as proof that zero waste manufacturing indeed works and can be just as, if not more, successful than traditional manufacturing. The steps of sewing are mostly the same; it's the design process and cutting process that have to shift. We need the full scope of a job before we start - for example, we need to know how many pieces are going to be ordered, in what size, for what delivery timeline, in which fabric. This is of course what every other manufacturer needs, however we are much more attached to the details. For example - if a client wants a certain pattern and certain fabric, we may have to edit the pattern or order other fabric based on the size rule they want. This can add 4-6 weeks to production time waiting for fabric etc to be produced.

Ironically, most of the struggles we've faced have not come from the zero waste nature of our factory, but from working within the existing manufacturing system. Purchase orders, payroll, minimums, unpaid invoices, and the like are what really cause the struggles, not the designs!"

decodecodecode.com   decodemfg.com   @decodecodecode

Ask Lizzy

Q: Is zero waste patterncutting giving rise to a particular aesthetic?

A: It's been said by some that zero waste patterns "are all boxy and voluminous", which is not true but that's what some people think of when they hear zero waste.

Zero waste is a *way* of making patterns and designing, rather than a particular style of clothes, and can be used for all sorts of aesthetics. Zero waste cutting can be used for many *types* of clothes, including menswear, children's clothes, underwear, swimsuits, toys, backpacks and coats.

Having said that, certainly technique can drive an aesthetic and zero waste can influence sewing techniques. For example, I've noticed I use facings far less now, and tend towards bias binding instead, either as a facing or binding (this means I also use interfacing less, as I don't need it for facings).

So yes, I guess it could indirectly influence an aesthetic in some ways.

Q: What kind of patterns should we be making zero waste?

A: For zero waste to have maximum effect, we should be using it for high-volume everyday clothes such as workwear, uniforms, jeans, etc, as these are where the biggest fabric savings will be made. Ironically, this is where it's hardest to adopt zero waste cutting. It's very hard to slot a zero waste model into the manufacturing setup we have at the moment. It's far easier for a one-person atelier to change or start-up as zero waste.

For my own zero waste patterns (which are for home sewing), part of me wants to make fabulously interesting cutting-edge avante garde fashions. However, the reality is that the patterns that sell the most are everyday clothes which are worn lots and sewn several times, and preferably have several variations, for example long or short sleeve options, tops which can be made dresses, and so on.

100

September

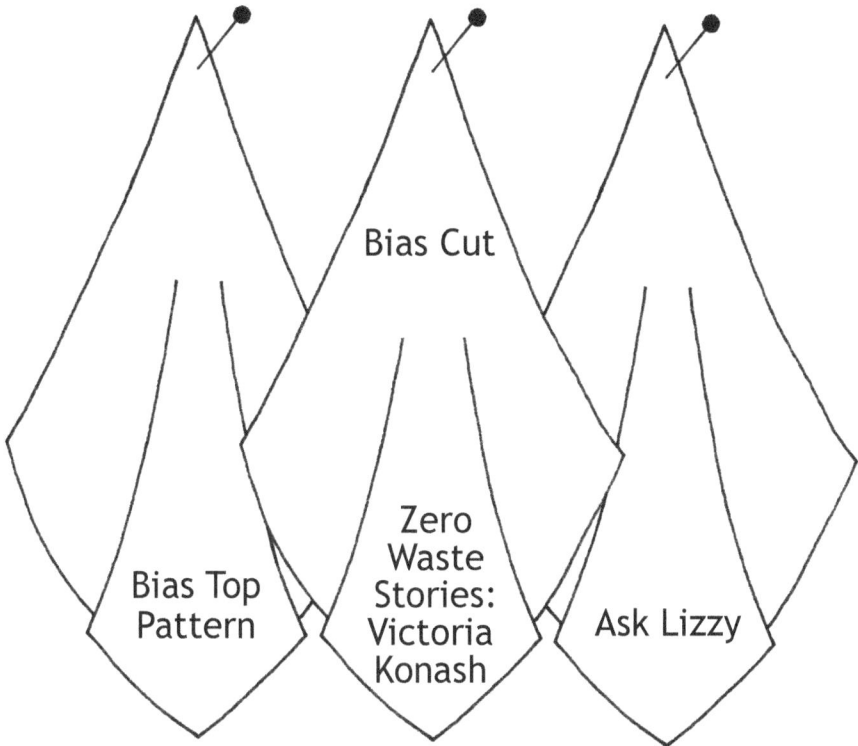

Bias Cut

Bias Top
Pattern

Zero
Waste
Stories:
Victoria
Konash

Ask Lizzy

Bias Cut
and zero waste

Bias cut clothes have a reputation for using more fabric and creating more scraps than those cut on the straight grain, and in most cases this is true. Typically, regular pattern pieces are used and a new 45° grainline is drawn on the pattern. When these are placed on the fabric, there are often unused triangle-y shapes around the edges.

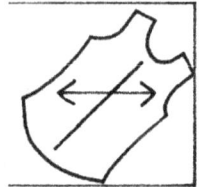

However, zero waste bias cut clothes have the potential to use even less fabric than regular non-bias cut patterns.

Bias cut has some great advantages. There's no need for bust darts, even for very large busts, and (depending on the fabric) the garment has the elasticity and flexibility to fit a variety of body shapes.

An obvious approach to creating a zero waste bias cut pattern is to position pattern pieces at 45 degrees, using up the spaces in between to avoid waste, just like how you'd plan a straight-grain zero waste layout. Often there's no way to make the garment longer (because the piece is placed diagonally and there's no room to add), so allow extra hem allowance if you need to vary the length.

Spiral cuts have the seams sewn on the straight grain with the garment hanging on the bias.
This involves thinking less about "back" and "front" and more about how the fabric can wrap around the body. It can take a bit of a mind-shift from how you may have been trained and how most clothes are made today.

Spiral cuts typically begin as a rectangle, are changed to a parallelogram, and then transformed by sewing it into a bias cut tube. Following are some ways you can do this - I recommend trying them out as paper models first.

Spiral cut - large triangle method. **1.** Begin with a rectangle. **2.** Fold one corner down so it touches the adjacent side and cut along the crease. **3.** Bring this triangle to the opposite end and sew it on, taking a minimal seam allowance eg 1cm/⅜". Overlock and press open - you now have a parallelogram. **4 & 5.** Pin, then sew the two long sides together, matching A-A and B-B. Note that one of the sides will be 1cm/⅜" shorter due to the seam you sewed in Step 3 - start matching the seam at the bottom and leave the overhang at the top. **6.** Finished tube with spiral seam.

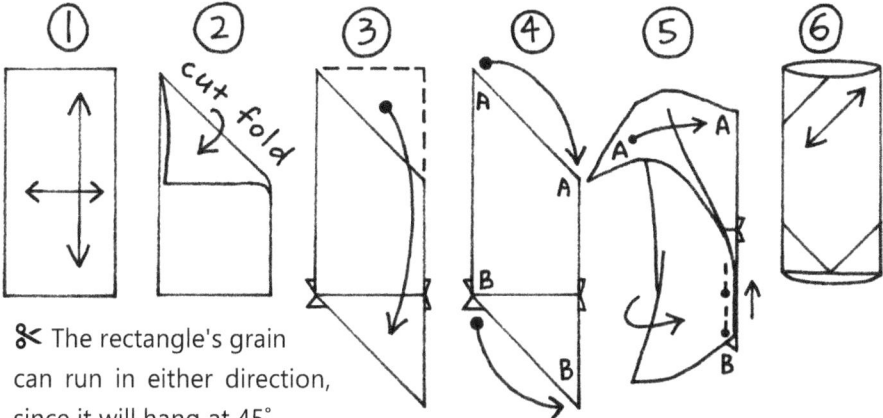

✂ The rectangle's grain can run in either direction, since it will hang at 45°.

Wait up - how big do I cut the starting rectangle?

First decide the *finished* dimensions of the tube. To find the rectangle's **width**, *divide* the finished width (+ 2 seam allowances) by 1.414. To find the rectangle's *length*, *multiply* the finished length by 1.414.

Note that the finished length won't be exact - the weight and drape of the fabric, and how it drops on the bias, will all affect the length. Finalise the length when you try the garment on.

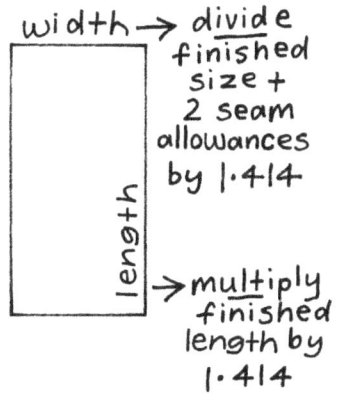

width → divide finished size + 2 seam allowances by 1.414

length → multiply finished length by 1.414

I'm a maths nerd. How is it calculated?

The key is Pythagoras' $a^2+b^2=c^2$.

For the rectangle's **width**, look at the triangle you cut off in Step 2. The hypotenuse (**c**) is on the bias and will become the finished circumference of the tube. The other 2 sides (**a** and **b**) are the same length, so you could write the equation as $a^2+a^2=c^2$ or $2a^2=c^2$. Then re-arrange the equation to discover **a**, which will be the width of the starting rectangle.

$$a^2 + a^2 = c^2$$
$$2a^2 = c^2$$
$$a^2 = \frac{c^2}{2}$$
$$a = \frac{\sqrt{c^2}}{\sqrt{2}}$$
$$a = \frac{c}{\sqrt{2}}$$
$$a = \frac{c}{1.414}$$
$$a = c \div 1.414$$

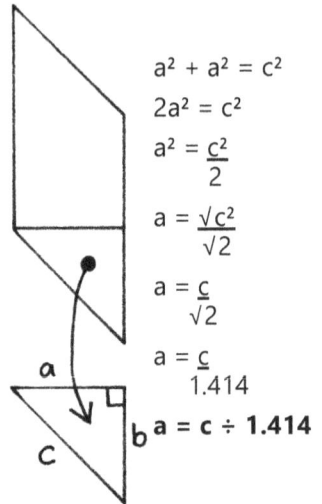

$$a^2 + a^2 = c^2$$
$$2a^2 = c^2$$
$$\sqrt{(2a^2)} = c$$
$$\sqrt{2}a = c$$
$$1.414a = c$$
$$\mathbf{1.414 \times a = c}$$

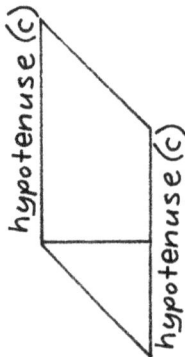

For the rectangle's **length**, look at the long sides of the parallelogram. These become the spiral seam that winds around the tube, hanging on the 45° after sewing. Therefore, the spiral seam gets treated like a giant hypotenuse, becoming **c** in the equation. **a** is the finished length of the bias tube. Re-arrange the equation to discover **c**, since **a** is your desired finished length.

Spiral cut - 2 triangle method. Another (favourite!) way to make a parallelogram. **1.** Begin with a rectangle. **2 & 3.** Fold in half longways, right sides together, and sew across the short ends with any seam allowance. **4.** Press seams open or to one side. Fold as shown. **5.** Cut *opposite* diagonal folds. **6.** Open out to reveal a parallelogram. Follow Steps 4 & 5 on the previous page.

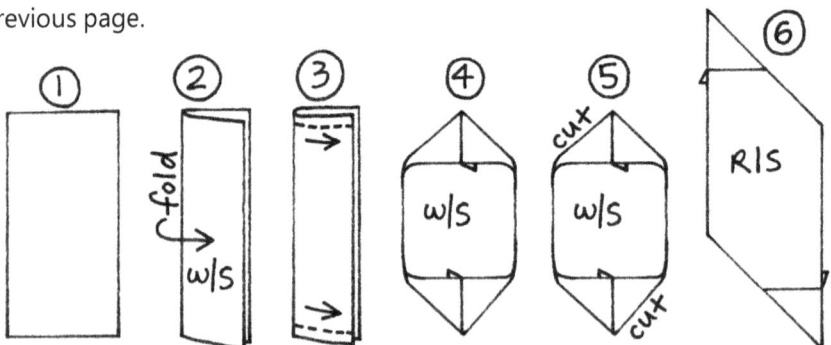

Spiral cut - one end closed. **1.** Begin with a rectangle. **2.** Fold it in half longways, right sides together, and sew across the short ends. **3 & 4.** Open it out and cut *one* of the diagonal folds. **5.** Lay the top triangle part flat and position the seam *exactly* in the centre (measure it!). Bring the longest edge (the one with the triangle sewn on the end) across and pin the raw edges together starting at X. **6-8.** Flip the whole thing over and continue pinning the raw edges. Keep on going until you reach the end. Sew, overlock and press. **9.** This was the basis for the Madame Grès envelope dress of 1961 and also a zero waste pattern of mine, the Xanthea dress.

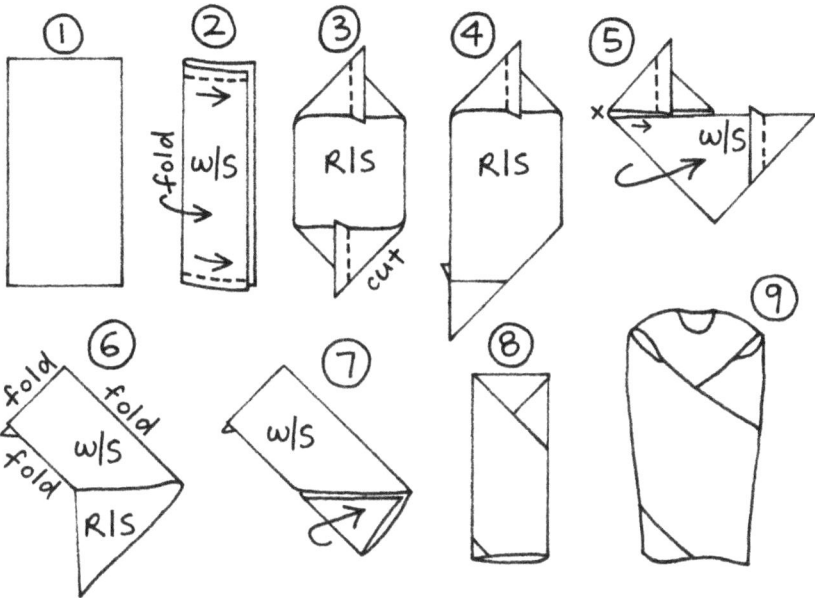

If you're a weaver, it's possible to weave diagonal ends, thus reducing the number of seams needed. Make a template of the diagonal to lay on your loom as you weave, to get the angle right.

A bias cut tube can be used in a variety of ways.
You can use it as-is, and create bias cut skirts, tops and dresses by cutting armholes, creating collars, etc. Pleat, dart or gather sections to fit the body. You'll need at least 10cm/ 4" ease, or up to 18cm/7" for fabrics that drop a lot on the bias, as the more a fabric drops, the narrower it gets.

A bias tube can also be used to create a bias fabric and then pattern pieces laid on top to cut out. Indian Churidar trousers (low waste) are cut using this concept. →

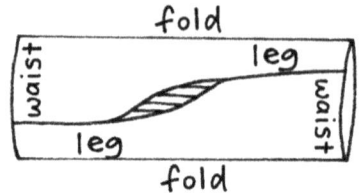

This opens up big worlds of possibility with zero waste layouts. You could using an existing straight-grain layout and cut the whole garment on the bias. The idea could be used to cut parts of a garment on the bias.

For example, you could cut bias sleeves.

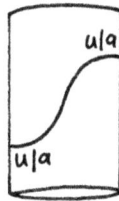

Or patch pockets with pointy flaps.

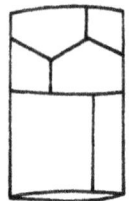

You could create bias fabric from long lengths of fabric or theoretically even whole rolls. 115cm/45" wide fabric will yield a tube approx 160cm/63" in circumference, and 150cm/59" will yield 212cm/83½".

4 Tips for Bias Cut

✂ Fabric choice can dramatically affect the look of the garment. Floppy, fine and loosely-woven fabrics will drop more on the bias, giving a fluid garment. Crisp fabrics give a totally different silhouette and can look fab. I suggest using stable fabrics such as cotton lawn for first garments.

✂ If you make a bias tube, and need to store it before cutting it into a garment, don't hang it up or it will stretch - store it folded flat.

✂ If the garment ends up too long, save what you cut off the bottom. You'll have a length of bias cut fabric ideal for bias binding, piping or trim.

✂ Experiment with how you're going to finish armholes, necklines and so on. Stabilise them if they're on the bias as you want to arrest stretching. I favour 6mm/¼" cotton tape but strips of fusing, strips of selvedge or folded bias strips of fabric may be suitable too. Experiment with seam and hem finishes as well.

Make a Bias Cut Wraparound Halter Top

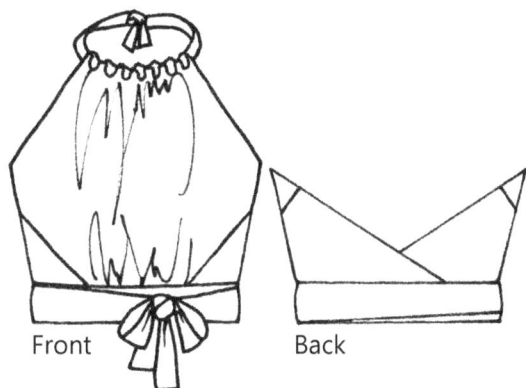

Front   Back

This top is made from two squares of fabric, one for the outer and the other for the lining. Attach a skirt to transform it into a dress. Suitable fabrics include soft wovens such as quilting cotton, lawn and babycord.

A YouTube sew-a-long is here: www.youtube.com/watch?v=wo9IGjQ_qZ8

You need:

✂ **2 perfectly cut squares of fabric.** See the following page for the dimensions. Choose a size according to your bust measurement, then check the finished centre front (CF) length (excludes waistband). Note there's a full bust adjustment for sizes bust 44"+. The two squares don't have to be the same colour or even the same fabric, as one is for the lining and remains hidden.

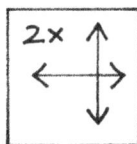

✂ A strip of fabric for the **waistband**, which can be the same or a contrasting fabric. **Width:** 7cm/2¾"-12cm/4¾". **Length:** twice your waist + 80cm/31½".

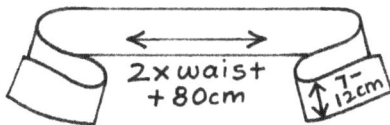

✂ Ribbon or self-fabric **tie for the neck**. It needs to be "grippy" ie grosgrain ribbon rather than satin, otherwise the channel it goes through will slip and not stay in place.

Finished size: 1.5cm/⅝" wide x 115cm/45" long.
For a self-fabric one, *cut* it 5cm/2" wide and sew it as a tube.

107

Your bust	Cut square	CF length
76.2cm/30"	50.5cm 19⅞"	31.7cm/12½"
81.2cm/32"	51.4cm/20¼"	32.3cm/12¾"
86.3cm/34"	52.3cm/20½"	33cm/13"
91.4cm/36"	53.2cm/21"	34.9cm/13¼"
96.5cm/38"	54.1cm/21⅜"	34.2cm/13½"
101.6cm/40"	55cm/21⅝"	34.9cm/13¾"
106.6cm/42"	55.9cm/22"	35.5cm/14"
	56.8cm/22⅜"	36.1cm/14¼"
	57.7cm/22¾"	36.8cm/14½"
	58.6cm/23"	37.4cm/14¾"
111.7cm/44"	59.5cm/23⅜"	38.1cm/15"
116.8cm/46"	60.4cm/23¾"	38.7cm/15¼"
121.9cm/48"	61.2cm/24¼"	39.3cm/15½"
127cm/50"	62.1cm/24½"	40cm/15¾"
132cm/52"	63cm/24⅞"	40.6cm/16"
137.1cm/54"	63.9cm/25⅛"	41.2cm/16¼"
142.2cm/56"	64.8cm/25½"	41.9cm/16½"
147.3cm/58"	65.7cm/25⅞"	42.5cm/16¾"
152.4cm/60"	66.6cm/26¼"	43.1cm/17"
157.4cm/62"	67.5cm/26⅝"	43.8cm/17¼"

To sew

All seams 1cm/⅜"

W/S = wrong side

R/S = right side

1. (Do Steps 1 to 4 for both squares.)
Fold a square in half diagonally.

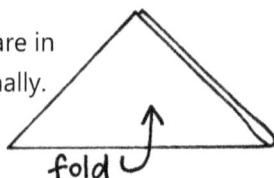

fold

2. Fold it in half again, leaving 1cm/⅜" showing of the tip of the triangle.

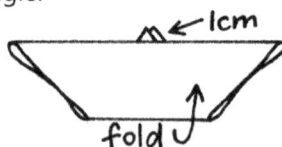

←1cm

fold

Press the folds with your fingers.

3. Unfold and cut along the top and bottom creases.

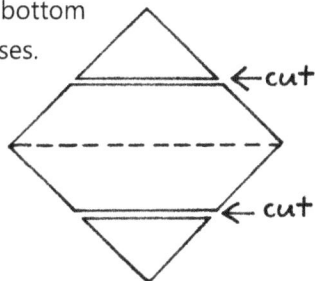

4. Sew the triangles onto the sides.

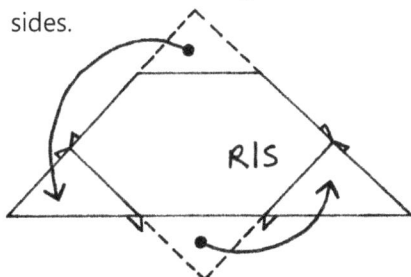

R|S

Press the seams open.

5. Place both shapes on top of one another R/S together and sew the sides, stopping 3cm/1¼" from the top. Press this bit open and stitch around.

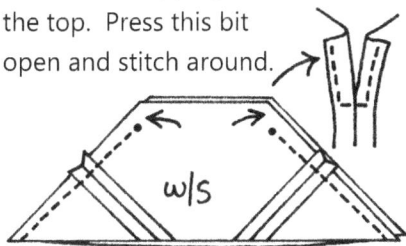

w|s

6. Sew across the top and turn through. Press.

w|s

7. Sew a 2cm/¾" wide channel along the top edge, and thread the tie/ribbon through.

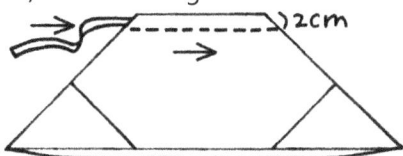

2cm

8. On the lower edge, gather between the seams, through both layers. Pull up the gathers to half the original distance.

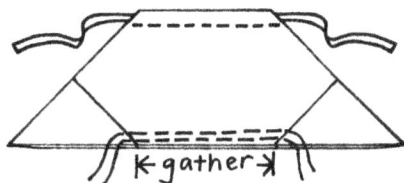

←gather→

✂ Are you making a dress? Sew the top up to this stage.

9. Press the band in half longways, *wrong* sides together.

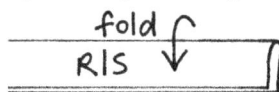

fold
R|S

10. Sew one long edge of the waist band to the top, R/S together. Press the seam towards the band.

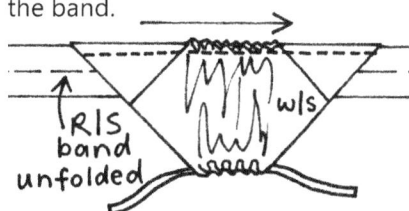

R|S
band
unfolded

w|s

109

11. Sew the ties right sides together, turn through and press.

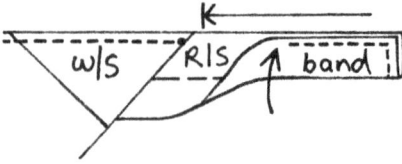

12. Fold the remaining edge of the waistband into place. Fold under the seam allowance and stitch by hand.

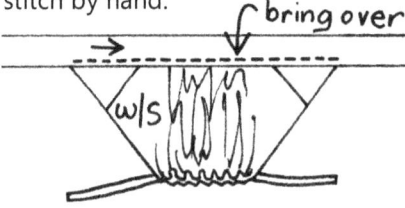

Run bust darts from the armholes if you have gaping at the sides.

Wrap dress version

A dress with a gathered skirt can be made by cutting a skirt and a slightly different waistband.

✂ Cut a rectangle for the skirt. Make the **width** 3 x your waist, and the **length** your choice.

✂ Cut 2 waistbands 5cm/2" wide, and the same length as you would for a top. Interface the central section the circumference of your waist.

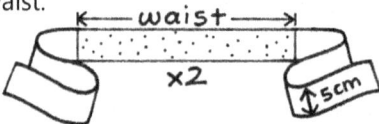

1. Hem the sides and lower edge of the skirt. Gather the skirt to 1.5 x your waist.

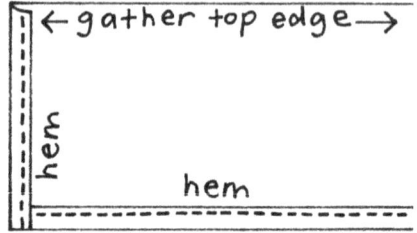

2. Sandwich the skirt's gathered edge between the two waistbands and stitch the entire length of the waistbands together.

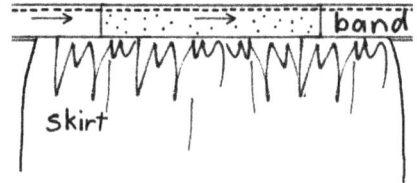

It's actually easier to do this in two stages: stitch one waistband on with the gathering uppermost, then the second one following the first line of stitching.

3. Make the top excluding Step 9, and join it to the centre of the waistband as described in Steps 10-12.

4. Try the dress on and see how far the ties wrap around your waist. Sew a buttonhole in the waistband to bring the underneath tie through.

110

✂ Note that any wraparound skirt pattern which wraps 1.5 times around the waist can be attached to the top. **Here's a gored skirt:**

1. On paper, draw a rectangle.
Length: 60cm/23⅝".
Width: (1.5 x your waist) divided by 7.

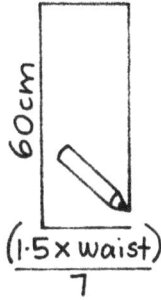
60cm

$$\frac{(1\cdot5 \times waist)}{7}$$

2. Add 12.7cm/ 5" to each side to make a trapezium.

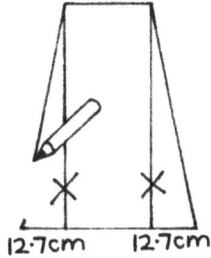
12·7cm   12·7cm

3. Curve the top and bottom edges: measure up 6mm/¼" at the top and 2cm/¾" at the bottom. The sides should measure 60cm/23⅝". Fold it in half to mirror the curves; the centre is the grainline.

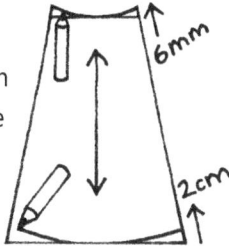
6mm
2cm

4. Add 1cm/⅜" seam allowances and a 2.5cm/1" hem. The curved hemline will not accommodate a hem deeper than 2.5cm/1".

Adjust the length by extending the sides on the same plane with a ruler.
Cut 5.

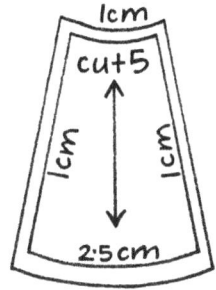
1cm
cut+5
1cm   1cm
2·5cm

5. Make the two end gores by tracing off the pattern you've just made and drawing a line parallel with the grainline, squaring off the lower corner to 90°. Add a 2.5cm/ 1" hem to the line. Cut 2 *as a pair*.

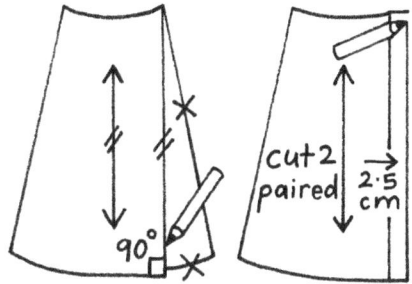
90°
cut 2 paired   2·5 cm

6. Cut the 7 gores out top-and-tailed with one another. You may need to cut across the fabric.

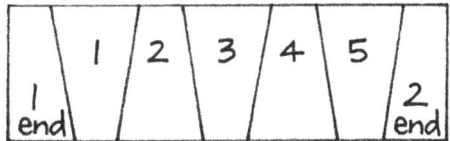
1   2   3   4   5
1 end   2 end

7. Sew together and hem.

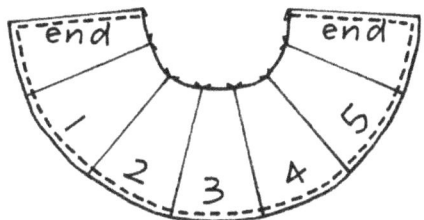
end   end
1   2   3   4   5

111

Victoria Konash of VixEco Design is a dressmaker, fashion designer and artist with broad experience in various crafts. She has been interested in fashion design as long as she can remember. Living in post-Soviet Belarus at the beginning of the 1990s, Victoria spent her teenage years with coupon systems and extreme shortages of anything in the empty shelf shops. She used to remake her family's unwanted old clothes into "new" skirts and dresses for herself. Although her initial university degree was in linguistics, Victoria never lost passion for fashion. She did some diploma courses in fashion design and patternmaking, studied at the London College of Fashion, and Open Colleges in Australia where she lives now. At present, Victoria teaches sewing and patternmaking skills, holds crafts workshops, designs and sells zero waste patterns and is also working on a #10zerowastedresses project and writing a book.

"I always wanted to make clothes. Both of my grandmothers were self-taught dressmakers, and watching them sewing and repairing for the entire village they lived in I knew I wanted to do the same. From an early age I tried to practice a zero to low waste approach, not because it was "trendy" to do so, but because back then all the materials were scarce and hard to get, so I tried to use and then reuse as much as I could putting close to nothing into the bin. About three years ago I came across a new-to-me concept: zero waste fashion design. I felt a strong connection to this method of patternmaking straight away and was amazed by the new opportunities and challenges so much

Zero Waste Stories

112

that I never went back to traditional pattern making and now 90% of my designs and patterns are zero waste.

All my designs start in my head as a silhouette or an idea; I do not sketch as such. I was pushed and encouraged to do so while studying fashion design, but I never felt this was my style. Instead, I imagine it in my head and straight away go to pattern drafting or draping. Most of my zero waste designs start with a traditional pattern block, which I manipulate around in my head, then on a piece of fabric to lock the pieces together as a jigsaw puzzle. I use odd small offcuts as various design elements or try to eliminate them altogether.

At the moment I'm working on my first zero waste challenge - #10zerowastedresses project. I thought that the best way to learn zero waste pattern making skills is to start practising them! Most of the zero waste designs I saw at the beginning of my journey were kind of square wide shaped garments, and I want to create something more elegant and sophisticated to prove that zero waste doesn't have to compromise the look. Right now I am up to number nine, and the designs have been getting more and more complex.

I often get asked *What does your business do?* I have to confess – I do not run a business. I used to. But about three years ago I decided to step away from a traditional business model and switch to a donations-based approach to work with people. I will be honest – I do not make money from what I do now. I do get paid for various community events, classes and workshops I run, but most of the payments go towards developing my future projects and supporting my family.

So what do I do if not business? I live my dream. I teach, I hold craft workshops for various communities, I do clothes repairs and alterations in our local area for a donation, and I design sewing patterns. And my online shop follows the same model – I offer people to choose how much they can afford to pay for my designs and sewing patterns. Offering my work from my heart, I simply ask people to pay from their heart what they can. I do make clothes, as I always wanted to as a child, but for now only for myself, my family and very close friends."

www.vixecodesigns.com   @victoriakonash

Ask Lizzy

Q: I have a fashion business and would like to be zero waste. How would I even begin?

A: If you're planning to transition to zero waste, and you have staff, make sure *everyone* understands what you want to do and is on board with it. Otherwise it's too easy to override zero waste with other concerns. It could end up like a household trying to go zero waste where one person doesn't understand or care about it and unwittingly sabotages everyone else's efforts.

Minimal waste can be the stepping stone to zero waste. Start with some easy victories: look at the patterns you already have and see where you can make some changes to the shapes to fit them together better on the layout. Sometimes it can be as small as adding an extra seam. Are all your cutting layouts generated automatically by computer? Investigate this - manually made ones will generally save more fabric and if the pattern pieces have been designed to fit together with minimal or zero waste, the person who made the pattern will be better at layouts than the computer.

Share your progress with your customers. Tell them what you are trying to do and what you have achieved, and what you will be working towards next.

Q: To make a zero waste pattern, what's a good item to start with?

A: Try an accessory such as a bag. It won't take much fabric and doesn't require grading. If you already have a non-zero waste bag pattern, you can use it as a starting point.

Garment-wise, skirts are fairly easy because they're essentially a tube shape with no armholes or crotch curves to worry about. They're simpler to grade multiple sizes, too.

October

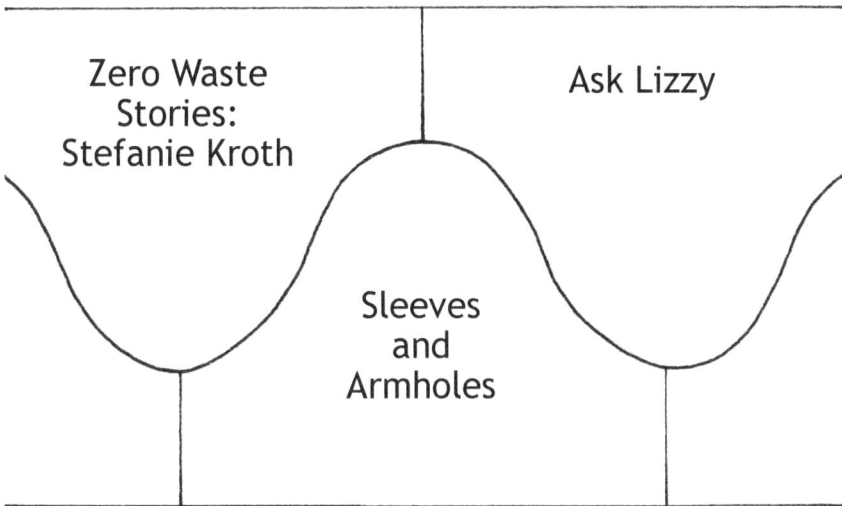

Zero Waste
Stories:
Stefanie Kroth

Ask Lizzy

Sleeves
and
Armholes

Sleeves and Armholes

One of the hardest parts of designing zero waste tops is getting a good close-fitting armhole and sleeve.

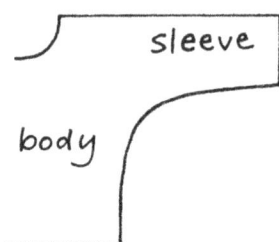

The easiest type of sleeve to make is an extended sleeve, where the body and sleeve are cut in one. Sometimes these have an underarm gusset for more movement, and other times they're so loose-fitting it doesn't matter.

Balenciaga favoured these minimally-seamed sleeves.

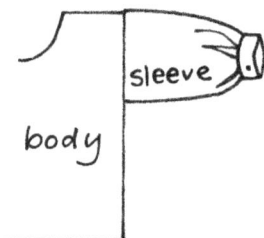

The next easiest type of sleeve belongs in a square-cut garment, where the armhole is a slit in the seam and the sleeve is a rectangle. These sometimes have underarm gussets too.

But what if you're pursuing a classic armhole and sleeve shape?

Every zero waste patternmaker's dream!

See if you can nest the sleeve's curves into other areas of the garment. For example, sometimes sleeve heads can be fitted into shirt tails, or a flatter sleeve head can fit into the shoulder slopes. With these, note that sleeve widths don't increase at the same rate as bodies, so the space around the sleeve will increase as the sizes get bigger.

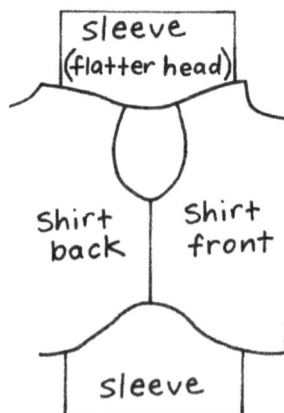

116

Tessellating the sleeve head

This will give you options for fitting the sleeve heads together with themselves. It gives a sleeve head that's symmetrical and works well for knits. It's okay for wovens too except very fitted sleeves. Add seam allowances before tessellating. Afterwards, check that it fits in the armhole.

1. Draw in the width of the sleeve and the height of the sleeve head. Mark the underarm (u/a) points and the top. The top is in the centre. **2.** Connect the underam and top with a ruled line. **3.** Mark the halfway point (A). **4.** Draw in a curve for one side. **5.** Trace the curve on a piece of tracing paper. **6.** Flip the tracing paper over and lightly colour the reverse side of the line (you're making your own carbon paper). **7.** Put the tracing back over the curve, then pivot it on point A and draw it in the other side. (If you're using CAD, simply copy the curve and rotate it on point A.) **8.** Review the curved shape. **9.** When you're happy with the shape, fold the paper in half and cut both sides together so it's mirrored. **10.** Finished sleeve. **(a) & (b)** The curve in Step 4 doesn't have to be even - you can draw any crazy shape and it will still tessellate.

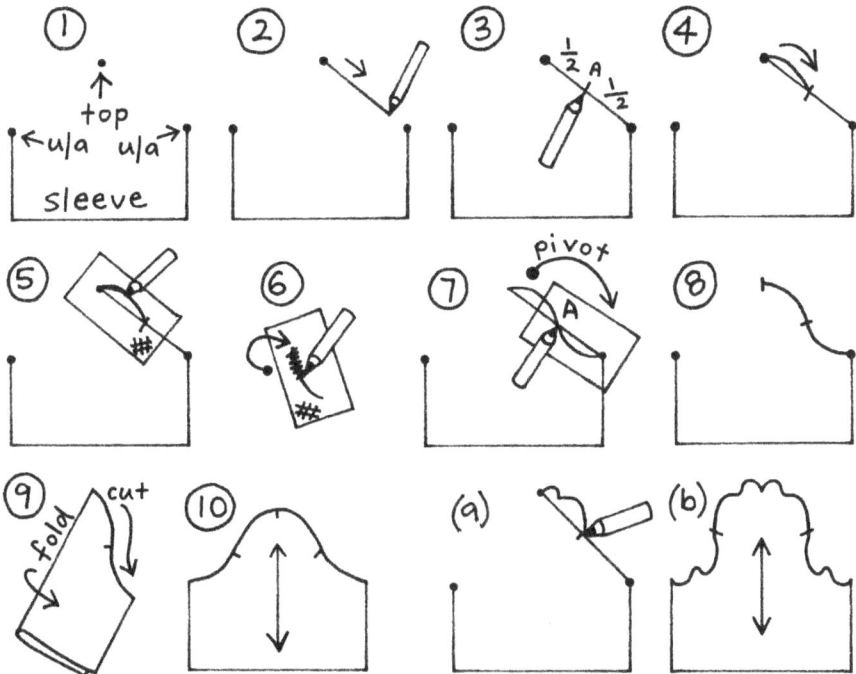

Tessellated sleeves have a few drawbacks:

✂ The sleeve head is symmetrical, so you won't get the nuanced fit of different front and back curves.

✂ The underarm is a little more scooped out than a classic sleeve block.

✂ With grading big sizes, sleeve heads tend to change proportions and become more asymmetrical, so you may have fit issues.

However, there are many ways you can arrange a tessellated sleeve.

If you're cutting lots of sleeves, they can fill the width of the fabric. There'll be half sleeves on the ends - these will need a central seam, or you could make *all* the sleeves with a central seam. Note in the arrangement below that the half sleeves don't make a *pair*; they're the same shape rotated.

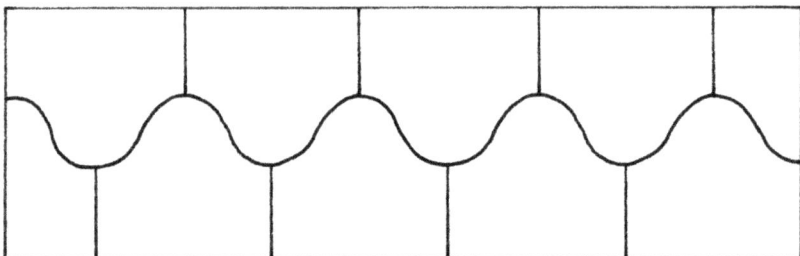

For a single set of sleeves, a central seam will allow the pieces to be cut like this. →

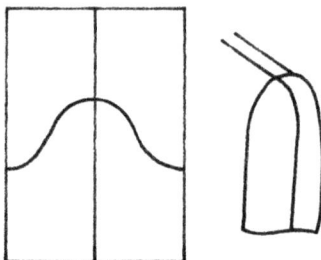

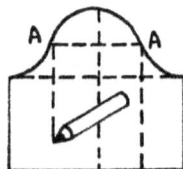

If you draw some lines on your sleeve pattern, they can be used as a guide to re-arranging the pieces.

Do you still have point A marked on the pattern from tessellating? Horizontally connect points A-A (dividing the sleeve head in half) and the two underarm points.

Vertically, draw in the centre line and down from each point A.

118

Create a seam from points A-A, and then a central seam. Invert the pieces to create a modular shape.

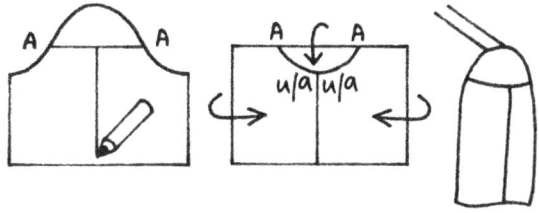

You could reverse this and put the central seam in the sleeve head instead of the arm.

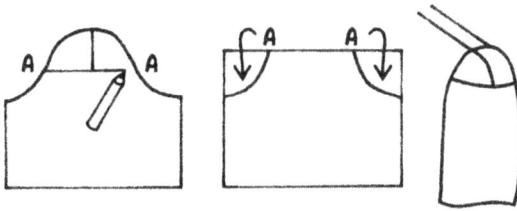

There doesn't have to be a seam in the centre of the sleeve; it can be moved off to the side, either to the front or back. Draw a vertical line down from point A, to divide the sleeve into ¾:¼. Cut along the line and move the smaller piece to the other side. The sleeve will tessellate with itself, but note that this *doesn't produce a pair* of sleeves.

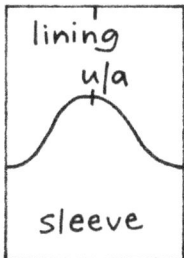

A sleeve with a self-lining can be cut nested with itself to create a modular shape. The outermost layer will have a regular underarm seam, and the lining will have a central seam.

✂ After slicing up the pattern, **remember to add seam allowances** where necessary.

Tapering a sleeve

Arms aren't tubular, they're tapered (except for babies arms), and most sleeves are tapered to match the arm.

Note that the angle of the sides of the sleeve will get steeper as you grade to bigger sizes.

If you have a tessellated sleeve head and need multiple sleeves, the arms can be marked separately from the sleeve heads. This gives more sleeve heads than you need, so mark out enough of each to give whole sleeves.

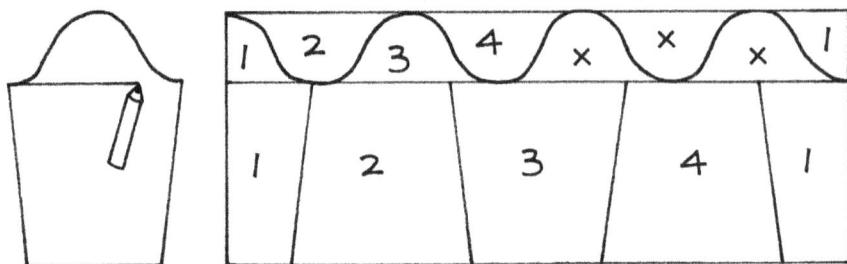

Historical patterns use a variety of ways to taper sleeves. On square-cut garments, a very easy way to make tapered sleeves is to have a central seam and top-and-tail the sleeve pieces.

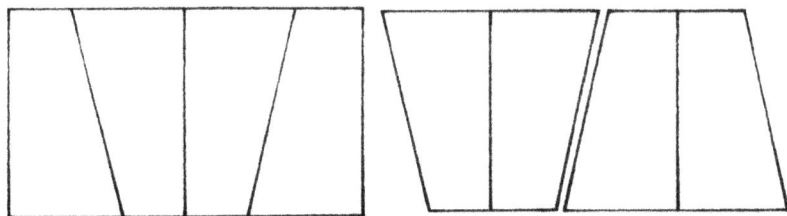

Instead of a central seam, you could cut a triangular wedge off one side and sew it onto the side of the *other* sleeve. The nap on the triangles will run in the opposite direction, but positioned on the back it isn't noticeable.

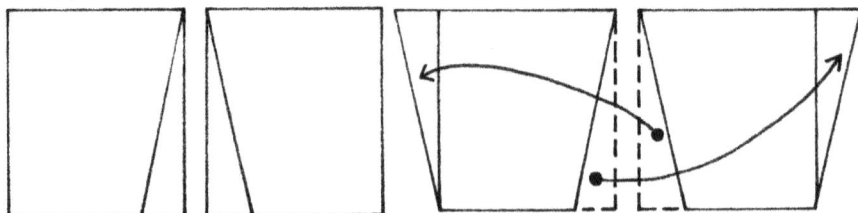

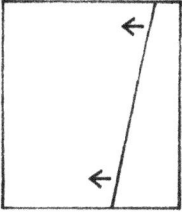

The wedge doesn't have to be triangular - it could have 4 sides and be cut closer to the centre of the sleeve. This makes a less-messy junction than a triangular point.

I've tried this idea with a tessellated, tapered sleeve block with semi-success.

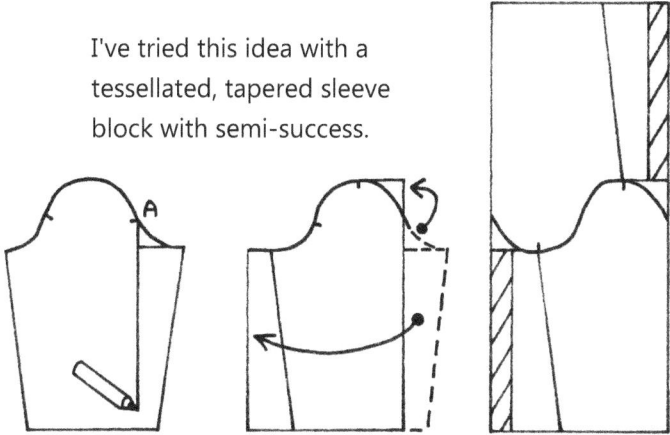

Sometimes historical patterns cut a triangle off at the wrist and sew it on further up the sleeve, to give a tapered shape.

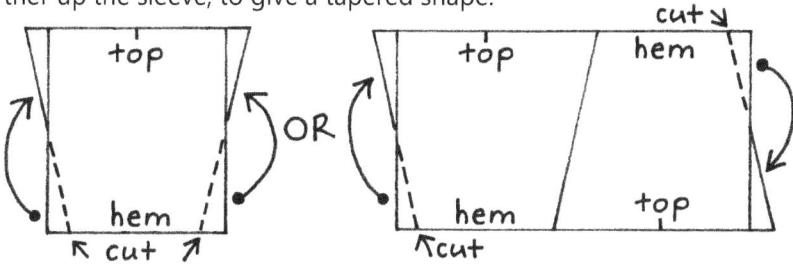

top

hem

⤤ cut ⤢

OR

top

hem

⤤cut

cut ⤵

hem

top

Sleeves can also be tapered using sewing. For example: tucks, darts, dart & placket, or gathers/pleats.

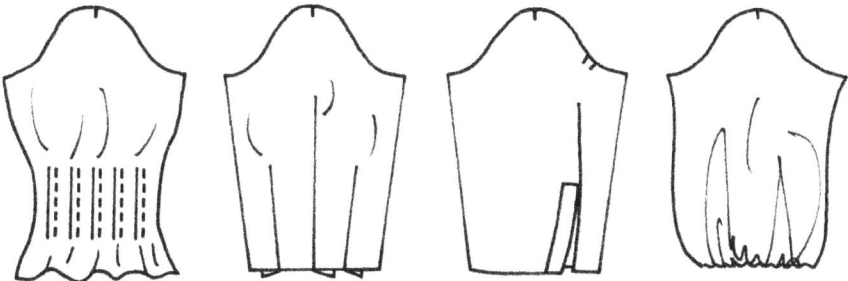

121

What about 2-piece sleeves?

Two-piece sleeves, the sleeve of choice for jackets, involve more curves and are trickier to fit into zero waste layouts. Sometimes they are cut *across* the grain (with the body pieces cut the regular way).

To create a square-er shape, sometimes the back armhole of the undersleeve is nested with the top sleeve.

The undersleeve could be cut straighter and curved with a dart.

BE BOLD!
Zero waste is an opportunity for creativity

We have an opportunity to design really interesting sleeve shapes, via patternmaking, which wouldn't come about in other ways.

Some thoughts:

✂ Maybe you have some unusual shapes in your cutting layout which you could try as sleeves.

✂ You can change the silhouette by putting the armhole/s in an unexpected place. This can give unusual asymmetrical silhouettes.

✂ The armhole could be an oval, circle, slit, teardrop or another shape.

✂ Can you draw a sleeve pattern or armhole freehand?

✂ Cut all or part of the sleeves on the bias.

✂ Be informed by what the fabric is capable of. Consider volume and how to create it.

✂ Trouser and sleeve shapes have a lot in common - can you transfer cutting concepts from one to the other?

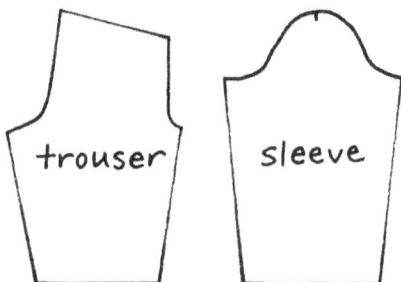

A gallery of armhole cutouts

A sleeve must have a armhole in which to sew it! Armholes can vary dramatically in shape, proportion and size, and the negative space they leave in a layout is an opportunity for creative details. You can even design armhole shapes to get the design detail you want.

Gather an edge and use it to add volume underneath gathers. ↓

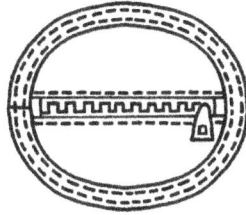

← Oval shaped armholes make oval pockets, with zips or welts for the opening.

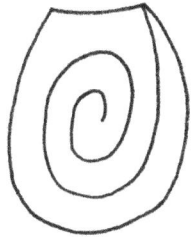

← Cut the shape in a spiral to use for little frills or flowers.

A bib front on a top or dress. →

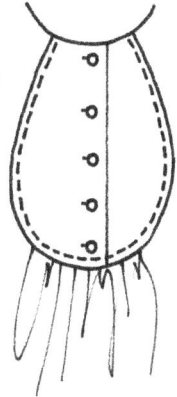

←Patch pockets. The cutout can be pressed around a cardboard template for a uniform pocket size.

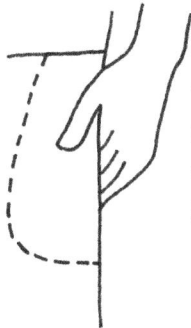

←Pocket bags. On small sizes these will be very little!

Create a ruffle of some sort. →

Plackets. → For cuffs, fronts, flys, or any opening.

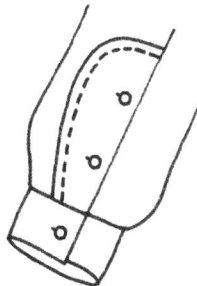

The cutout can be used for reinforcing garment areas → eg knees, elbows, shoulders, thighs.

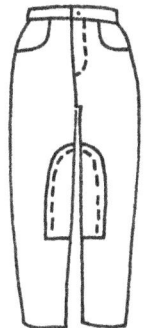

123

STEFANIE KROTH

Stefanie Kroth is a freelance pattern technician. She makes patterns in CAD, does grading, 3D fitting (in CLO 3D) and markers. Her clients are fashion labels and made-to-measure manufacturers as well as creators of sewing instructions or books. She works mainly digitally on various computers in her Bavaria-based studio, alongside regular equipment such as sewing machines, cutting tools and dressmaker's mannequins. She is the author of *Zero Waste Nähen* (Stiebner, 2022).

Stefanie has been sewing since she was a teenager out of a growing curiosity in making garments that didn't exist or were unaffordable. This was followed by an apprenticeship in a fashion college (Modefachschule Sigmaringen) and a degree in Media and Communication (University Augsburg). Stefanie pursued various internships and freelance work, such as for Pam Hogg (London), Schöffel Sportswear, Fashion Editorial of the magazine Brigitte (Hamburg), and costume design for theatre productions (Augsburg). Stefanie managed two of her own labels: *Rosenschön* and *SO! Pattern*, and worked for the made-to-measure labels Safiyaa, Befeni, and We are Dessousmakers. She also taught at the POP-Academy for Fashion in Munich.

"I have long been interested in special, tessellated patterns with unusual seams and a better fit to get the most out of the fabric. When I discovered *Zero Waste Fashion Design* by Holly McQuillan and Timo Rissanen and went to a Creative Cutting Conference, the dam broke. I realized, 'I'm not alone!' There are other people who are and have been dealing with these issues.

124

I started by recreating everything I found on zero waste fashion as mini-models or re-sewing and adapting. In the process, I also discovered the tremendous variety with zero waste design and was completely hooked.

When I design zero waste patterns, I return to analog techniques, like mini mockups of paper, draping on the mannequin and working with real fabrics. The beauty of zero waste is the combination of digital with tactile. Zero waste design brings demands with it such as catering to variable fabric widths, creating gradations for more complex patterns, or nesting different sets of sizes. With these, I'm looking for digital solutions, and continuously working in dialogue and exchange with other patternmakers.

My book, *Zero Waste Nähen* (the title translates as *Zero Waste Sewing*), shares this enthusiasm with others. There are 25 different styles in two different size sets presented. The book is published in German with an English translation in the works. With starting a zero waste pattern book you are confronted with many questions: which fabric width? Which sizes? Are the patterns for self-drawing or as layout plan? It was most important to me to show that zero waste design can be simple, complex, sporty, festive, classic and cool – in fact, a guide, inspiration and tool for your own ideas.

Collaborations are at the core of my work, whether it's a DIY zero waste label that seeks grading support, a fashion label that wishes to implement a specific style, or zero waste designers planning a collaborative project.
I want to make zero waste patterns fit for apparel production and be able to respond quickly to changing requirements, such as fabric width changes, different seam allowances, grading styles. At the moment, zero waste involves too many entry burdens for smaller fashion labels. We need to change that! Furthermore, we still need to address that non-sewers have usually little idea about pre-consumer waste. Here we still need good storytelling to make zero waste patterncutting understood. I hope that zero waste design will soon represent the bigger part of my work than conventional design."

www.stefaniekroth.de   @stefanie_kroth

Ask Lizzy

Q: **When I use a printable zero waste pattern, consisting of the whole layout, and lay the pattern on top of the fabric, what about my fabric scissors? Should I be cutting through fabric *and* paper?**

A: Some people cut apart the paper pattern first with paper scissors, and others just lay the whole printable pattern on top of the fabric and cut through all layers with their fabric scissors.

Paper is more abrasive than fabric (the fibres are tougher and it contains minerals to stiffen it and adjust how it absorbs printing inks) and will dull fabric scissors quickly if you use them for paper. Cutting with dull scissors places stress on your wrist and hand, as well as being annoying.

What do *I* do? I have a dedicated pair of paper scissors which happen to be sharp enough to cut through fabric too, so I use those.

Q: **Lizzy, what inspired you to work with zero waste fashion?**

A: By chance, I read about zero waste patterns in the book *Shaping Sustainable Fashion* and then *Zero Waste Fashion Design*, and I immediately clicked with it. I was already a clothing patternmaker, with a 20+ years career in manufacturing behind me, and was familiar with the amount of fabric scraps that factories throw away. I can attest that even small factories throw out large amounts.

I badly want to see this change in the fashion industry, in my lifetime, and I can see the potential that zero waste patternmaking has. As well as addressing fabric waste, zero and minimal waste patterns are much more economical on fabric, so we are using fewer resources in the first place.

I've always been somewhat passionate about patternmaking, and now I'm keen to see how far we can take zero waste towards transforming how clothes are made and changing the systems in the fashion industry.

126

November

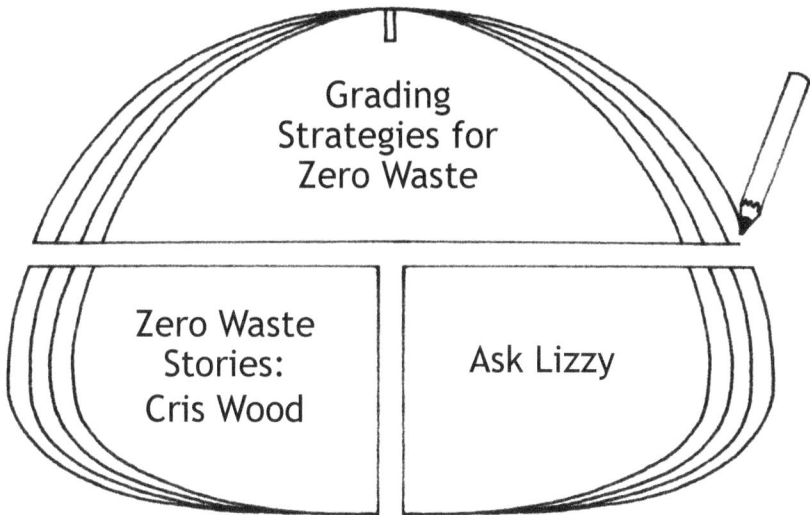

Grading
Strategies for
Zero Waste

Zero Waste
Stories:
Cris Wood

Ask Lizzy

Grading
Strategies
for zero waste

Grading, where we make all the sizes needed from a single pattern, can be a big sticking point with zero waste patterns.

You can understand the issue: with zero waste, the cutting layout IS the pattern, and if you make the pieces bigger, they won't fit on the fabric. If you make them smaller, there'll be gaps and it won't be zero waste anymore.

With regular patternmaking, the pattern pieces are graded *before* they're arranged in a cutting layout, and are independent of how they'll fit together. With zero waste, the grading needs to be considered and taken into account *as the layout is being made*. So unless you're only doing one size, you can't avoid it in the pattern planning.

There are many ways to go about grading, and even more ways to incorporate grading into a zero waste layout. Look at **how many sizes are possible within the layout**, and ask yourself **how many sizes do you want to be able to make?**

When we grade zero waste patterns, we're really just moving lines within the rectangle of the layout. We still need to remember how the body grows between sizes even if there are very unusually shaped pieces. I grade the largest pieces first and see where that leaves the smaller pieces.

These are some of the strategies I've had success with. Often I use more than one at a time.

1. Cut across the fabric

This breaks plenty of dressmaking rules! but it works well and I've used it often, especially early on. As garments grow in width rather than length (as the sizes increase) positioning pieces at 90 degrees to the usual way will give you the space to grade bigger - you just need more fabric. Often the fabric width will determine the garment's length. It does have a few snags: it's not suitable for every garment and fabric, for example knits, napped and directional prints, and you *must* be careful that the fabric doesn't shrink, because the garment will tend to get narrower before it gets shorter.

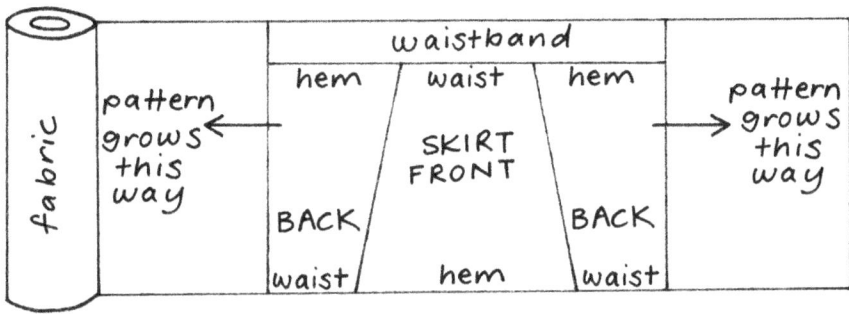

2. Modular pattern pieces

Modular pattern pieces are all squares and rectangles and can easily be moved around to fit on the fabric. Modular pattern pieces are an historic way to cut zero waste; the book *Cut my Cote* by Dorothy K Burnham (1973 Royal Ontario Museum) is full of these type of examples.

There are two ways to use modular pieces.

The first is if you're making **something small** such as underpants, bras, baby & children's clothes or bags. These things are never going to fit across the whole width of the fabric owing to their small size. Instead, make the pieces interlock so that the whole layout is rectangular, leaving useable rectangular scraps. The pattern can contain curves as long as the outside perimeter is squared.

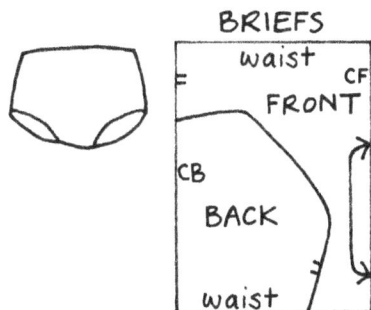

The second way is to make **pattern pieces that are modular and can be moved around the fabric**, accommodating different width fabrics and a big range of sizes. Again, this leaves useable rectangular scraps.

This is a good way to go if you're designing ready-to-wear clothes, because your cutter can mix-and-match sizes so you're using all of the fabric; the whole production run can be zero waste rather than striving for zero waste on individual garments. For home sewing patterns, where the person will only be making one at a time, I call this low waste or minimal waste.

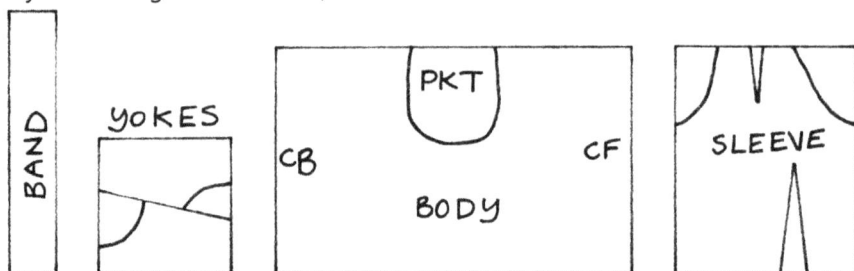

3. Sacrificial pattern piece

This is where a particular pattern piece gets smaller or changes position as the other pieces get larger.

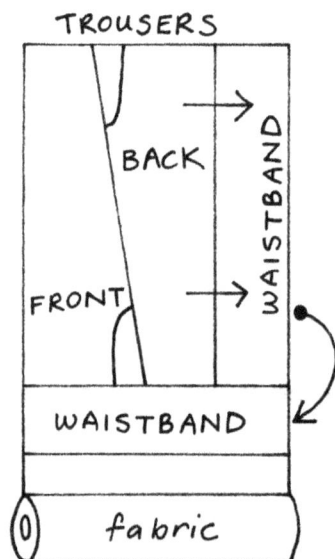

If you're using tessellating pattern pieces which interlock with themselves across the width of the fabric, they may or may not perfectly fit across the width. This is where a sacrificial pattern piece, such as a belt or tie, comes in handy to place in the empty area.

In this example with trousers, the waistband is sacrificial - as the trousers get wider, the waistband (or more than one waistband) changes width until it eventually disappears and is cut further down, across the fabric.

4. Sacrificial garment

This is a similar idea to having a sacrifical pattern piece, but this time a *whole garment* is sacrificial.   Position the main garment with another garment to make the pattern pieces fit better, and as it gets bigger, the second garment moves around or goes away. The second garment could be anything - a smaller size, an accessory, part of a matching set, etc.

In this example, a top is cut with a simple dirndl skirt. As the top increases in width, the skirt panels get narrower but extra panels are cut from more fabric. Each size skirt will have panel seams in different positions.

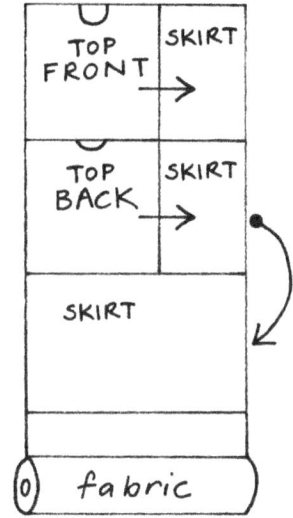

5. Grade the pattern pieces as normal, then make a new layout for each size.

This can be time consuming, and it's also difficult to do with the current patternmaking software. Sometimes I grade a few key pattern pieces as normal, then insert them into a new layout.

If you're creating PDF print-and-tape-together sewing patterns, this will result in a separate file for each size, because the cutting layout is the actual pattern for each size.

6. Change the fabric width

This is easier to do with home sewing patterns than production, because the fabric choice is in the maker's hands.

Use a wider width fabric for bigger sizes.   Sometimes you can make the pattern to fit 2 or even 3 fabric widths depending on the sizes you want to make.

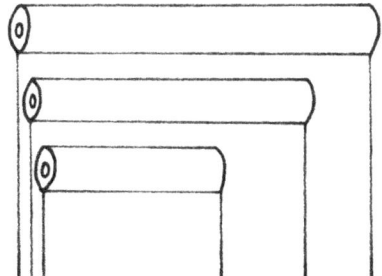

7. Consider a zero waste accessory

Why not try an accessory? Accessories such as bags don't need grading, but you can adjust the size by printing it out bigger or smaller.

Accessory making is a breeze compared with garments - you don't need to test-fit multiple sizes or find inclusive models...or any models!

I find it's easiest to make an accessory pattern starting with a non-zero waste pattern, to get the size and proportions right. Maybe you already have one you can use. Then take a look at the pieces and see where you can adjust the shapes to fit into one another to make a zero waste layout.

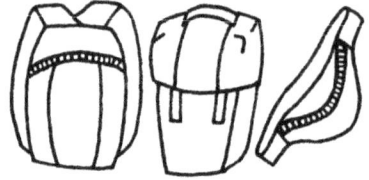

Extended sleeves

If your pattern has extended sleeves that fit across the width of your fabric, you can grade within the fabric width.

You may already know that long sleeves will conveniently fit within 150cm/59" width fabric, and short sleeves within 112cm/44". If you're doing this, I suggest leaving the selvedges at the wrists and just grade the body width, the underarm and the wrist width.

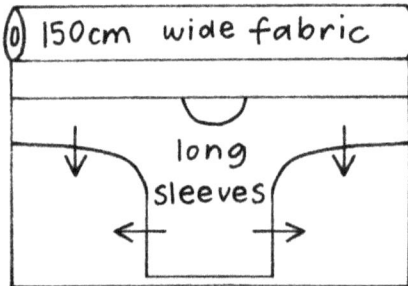

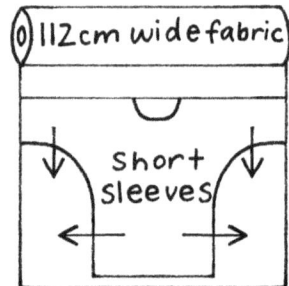

Grading bias cut clothes

If you have a garment that's cut on the straight grain but hangs on the bias, you need to grade it *as it hangs*, **not** how it's cut. For example, if your garment is constructed from squares which hang on the bias, calculate the grading as it's going to be worn on the body. You'll need to use Pythagoras's Theorem to find the width of the garment on the bias.

Bust darts

Do you need to add bust darts, increase the size of them, or do a full bust adjustment as you grade? This will obviously change your zero waste layout. Tops and dresses without darts will ride up at the front hemline, especially with large busts.

Note that there are some garments you can't put darts in, due to their cut. For example, the bog coat doesn't have any shoulder or side seams, making horizontal or vertical bust darts impossible.

Here are two solutions I use for bust darts in a zero waste pattern:

1. I make a bias cut garment. Bias cut clothes don't require bust darts, because the fabric hanging on the bias is flexible enough in both directions to fit over the bust. This works well even for very large busts.

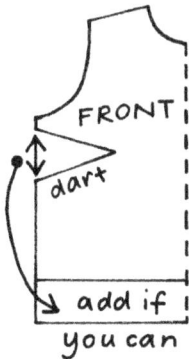

FRONT

dart

add if you can

2. When designing (home sewing) patterns, I allow an opportunity in the instructions to add bust darts, and arrange it so this is almost the last thing to do, with the garment completed enough so it can be tried on. The pattern needs at least 2cm/¾" side seams if not 2.5cm/1" to allow for the way the dart angles the side seam. It's easier if the seam allowances are overlocked separately first.

The garment is tried on and a dart pinned at each side until the hemline hangs straight. The dart needs to be as horizontal as possible and stop about 2.5cm/1" from the bust point. Then the garment is taken off, the darts evened up and then sewn. For large darts, they can be trimmed back to 1cm/⅜" and overlocked if necessary.

This creates a high-low hemline (which may work well for shirt tails) unless you have space to add onto the front length to compensate for the dart. The front side seam won't be straight at the dart location, however the wider seam allowance gives space to adjust the stitching line.

133

Big sizes, zero waste and test-fitting

It's taken me some years to get confident enough with zero waste to do it in bigger sizes, and I've gone bigger gradually.

The key, for me, has been **test-fitting**.

I know, that sounds time consuming and expensive, but the combination of zero waste and large sizes can give unexpected results, and you need your patterns to be right. It's very different from when I was an industry patternmaker, where we never used to test-fit beyond the sample; the pattern just got graded, end of story. However, we were only making five fashion sizes and not zero waste.

The good news is, it's unecessary to test-fit *every* size - that would take a long time and be wasteful. With zero waste, I started off test-fitting every third size, but now I test about every fifth. It partly depends on how easy-fitting the clothes are and how complex the pattern is. I try and test at least one size in each "decade" of inches - for example, I currently check sizes 36" bust, 46", 56" and 64" which are the sizes of the test models.

To test-fit, I ask friends or family in the approximate sizes I want to check. Sometimes I accost visitors. There are no modelling agencies out here in rural Australia! The best test fit models are honest and tell you exactly what they think, however brutal the truth is - you don't want filters and "yes men". Try to fit garments on as many different bodies as possible - the more you can test fit, the better picture you're able to build up of the fit.

While virtual modelling and dressmaker's mannequins will get you close regarding fit, and are good tools to use, at the end of the day there's no substitute for a real person, because they can talk.

When I test-fit, I make the test garment in a wearable fabric rather than calico, so it can be finished off and worn by someone. Some of the test-fit models are quietly building themselves a zero waste wardrobe in this way.

I try to get "double duty" out of the fit garments, if I can, so that they're used for more than just a fitting. I use them to check the sewing instructions as I make them. Sometimes I sew them in a stripe or a thicker fabric, for example, to see how a different fabric will look. Sometimes I end up using the fit garment for photography as well.

Other grading notes

✂ When you plan a layout and nest the pieces together, **consider the rate each piece will grow**. The pattern won't grade successfully if two pieces next to each other grow at different rates. For example, placing a side panel into a neckline will only work if you're doing a single size, because their growth rate is too different.

✂ For bigger sizes, **extra seams or little changes of style details may be needed** to fit the pieces on the fabric. To me, this is one of the quirks of zero waste and provided your customers understand what they're getting it shouldn't be a problem.

✂ **Build-in some ways the pattern can be adjusted**, as you're planning the layout, since zero waste sewing patterns aren't so easy to adjust. For example, deep hems, wider side seams, adjustable waists, and so on.

✂ **Three things that really help when I grade a pattern**
(any pattern, not just zero waste):

1. Try the garment on, if possible, and look in a full-length mirror. This will give you an idea of the proportions as it's being worn, and you'll see where to grade around pockets etc.

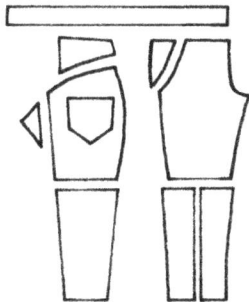

2. Arrange the pattern pieces on the table as they will be sewn together, like a puzzle. As with trying the garment on, you'll be able to see the proportions of the pieces in relation to each other, and plan your grading accordingly.

3. Record how you graded the pattern so that if you need to go back and make more sizes, it's all there. Make a sketch of the pieces and draw in the grade rules to refer to.

C
W

Cris Wood is the owner and sole designer of **Cris Wood Sews**, and is a California native now based in Seattle, WA, USA. She designs low-waste, size inclusive garment sewing patterns for beginners. Her focus is on sewist accessibility with the purpose of including sewists of all skill levels, sizes and shapes. To achieve this, Cris' patterns use only rectangular pattern pieces. The low-waste aspect of her patterns are naturally integrated into the creative multi-rectangular design. Rectangles are approachable for a beginner to draft, adjust, sew and lay out in a manner that leaves the smallest amount of fabric waste. The shape of the waste is always rectangular, so it can be used for other sewing projects. No paper pattern pieces are required, reducing paper waste as well. Her garments are defined by their relaxed nature. They allow the body to move comfortably through the world while maintaining a modern aesthetic free of embellishments.

"The way the sewing community has embraced my patterns has been so motivating. Everything about these patterns deviates from the norm. There is sometimes some education required for the experienced sewer who has a lot of standard pattern makes under their belt and are new to the self-drafting techniques involved. I am grateful for the adventurous sewist who is willing to engage in an unorthodox sewing experience.

I have always been an avid follower of fashion, both contemporary and vintage. Japanese designers in particular

Zero Waste Stories

136

excite me. The innovative and unconventional garments of the late Issey Miyake, Rei Kawakubo (Comme des Garçons) and Yohji Yamamoto top the list. When I am inspired by a design concept, I arrange rectangles in my head, letting them fold and bend in my mind's eye until something unique and accessible begins to take shape. Then, I sketch the idea wherever is convenient - the paper calendar in the kitchen, an envelope on the counter, and sometimes in the notebooks by my bedside or in the sewing room. Design ideas can "click" at any time, so I keep a pen at the ready for when a concept is solidified and ready to be made into a sample garment.

I get a lot of enjoyment from my work, but there are certainly challenges that come along with making these non-traditional patterns. I have been rejected from online sewing retailers because I cannot provide fabric requirements in a listing. In my patterns, exact fabric requirements vary considerably according to the unique measurements of the sewer, the formulas for which are provided in the pattern itself but are not conducive to a standard product listing. Representation in retail shops has also presented dilemas. Printing out individual patterns on paper would be contrary to my concept and my brand, so I am unable to reach sewists I would otherwise be able to.

I believe the concept of eco-friendly sewing to be deeply rooted in the DIY nature of sewing and the "use what you've got" attitude of earlier generations. Certainly re-use in the quilting community has long been in practice. I'm thinking particularly of the quilts of Gee's Bend, realized by using scraps and repurposing garments and textiles of all kinds to create functional works of art. I have seen a resurgence in the sewing community's interest in mending or reworking denim, dying garments to give them a second life and collecting scraps for the ever-popular patchwork styles.
The zero and low-waste patterns of today are an exciting addition to the traditional way we as sewists have been making our own clothes, and I am proud to stand alongside the designers who are creating them and the sewists who are embracing them."

www.criswoodsews.com   @criswoodsews

137

Ask Lizzy

Q: **What mistakes have you made with zero waste and what have you learned?**

A: One of the biggest mistakes I've made has been assuming that it wasn't possible to make some particular types of garments zero waste. Without even thinking it through, I sort of subconsciously wrote-off items such as bras, swimwear, underpants, hats and the like. However, other people didn't, and their work showed what was possible and has been an inspiration to me and others.

In mistakes with actual patterncutting, grading has been the most challenging area, expecially when I wanted to make many sizes. Some of the mistakes were hilarious - body lengths, armhole depths and proportions ended up crazy-looking!

Q: Are there any seam types and construction finishes more suitable for zero waste clothes than others?

A: I would say Yes, just going by my own work. A strong understanding of sewing, construction, and how fabrics perform is an advantage in fashion design generally, but I think more so with zero waste.

Zero waste makes you think hard about construction, sewing order and how areas will be finished off neatly (and easily!). As the pattern pieces are often unusually-shaped, so the construction might be unorthodox too.

In my own patterns, I rarely use facings anymore, preferring to finish edges in other ways such as binding, bias binding used as a facing, linings, and self-linings. I use bias binding so much I have a dedicated storage bin for it.

I try and cut garments with as few seams as possible (like Balenciaga!), such as front button stands that fold into place rather than are cut separately.

I'm increasingly thinking about longevity with construction: strengthening areas that get wear, making waistbands adjustable, and so on.

December

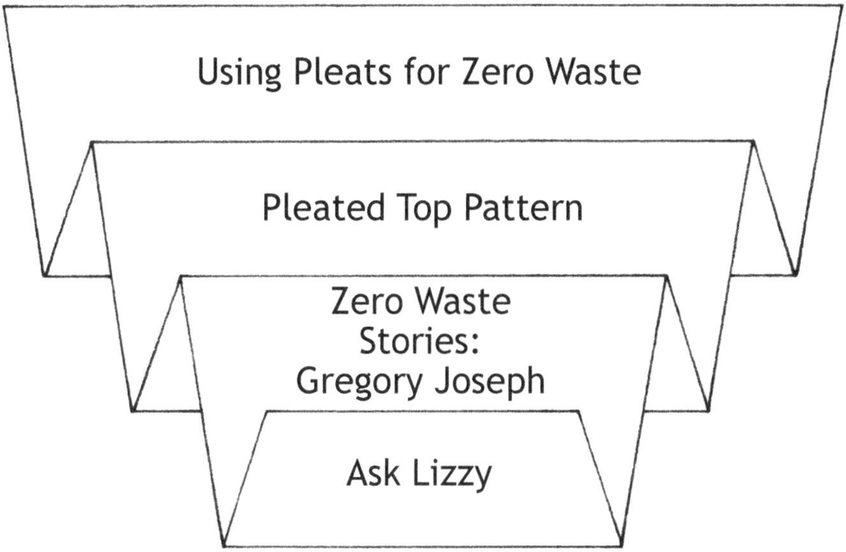

Using Pleats for Zero Waste

Pleated Top Pattern

Zero Waste
Stories:
Gregory Joseph

Ask Lizzy

Using Pleats
for zero waste

Pleats are one way to control fullness in fabric, alongside gathering, smocking, elastic, tucks, darts, ease, shirring and drawcords. Pleats can sometimes be used interchangeably with these.

While pleats don't sound like an obvious technique for zero waste, as pleating uses more fabric than unpleated cloth, pleats have some benefits: pleating triples the thickness of a garment and therefore makes it more opaque, warmer, possibly more durable, and avoids cutting the cloth.

Historically, pleating is preferable to cutting the cloth so the strength and integrity of the (handwoven) fabric isn't compromised. It also makes a garment adjustable by sewing extra/undoing some pleats, it makes it roomier to accommodate size changes and different body shapes, and potentially the fabric can be re-used. Additionally, it's less sewing work to create pleats than to cut, handsew and hand-neaten seams.

Pleats can be used...

1. **To make straight pieces curved**, if the pleats are tapered. Darts can do this too. This uses less fabric than seams. For example, the sides of a hat or the yoke of a skirt.

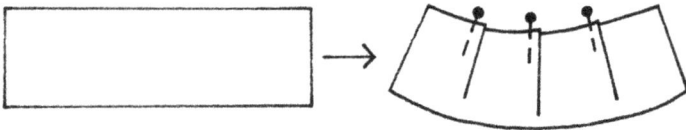

This idea could be used to pleat a piece of lace to create a pretty collar.

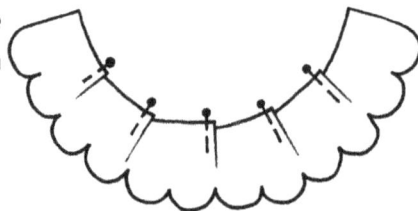

2. To create fullness which can be adjusted to suit the available fabric. All-round pleated skirts are a classic example, where the skirt is pleated according to the fabric width.

Fabric of varying widths can be pleated to a specific width and then a pattern laid on.

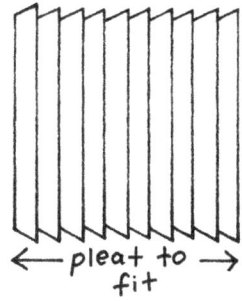

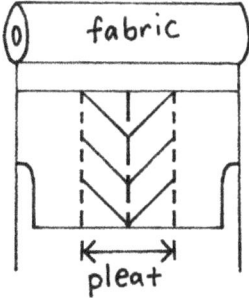

← pleat to →
fit

In this example, the fabric is pleated to fit the pattern, and the pleat depth can be adjusted to fit the fabric width.

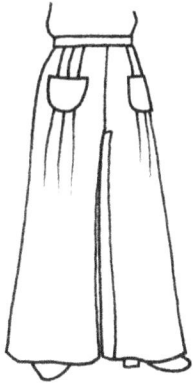

fabric

pleat

3. To make garment pieces which are close-fitting in some parts and flowing in others, without cutting the fabric. The fabric is typically pleated at the wrist, neckline, shoulders or waist.

English smocks, Regency square-cut shirts, smocked christening gowns, and early Scottish kilts (the Féileadh Mòr or belted plaid) all use this idea.

4. For garment longevity.
An historical example is stitched pleats around the hemline of a skirt, to be unpicked as a child grows taller.
Sometimes floor length skirts were made with the same stitched pleats, and as the hem of the skirt wore out, it was cut off and a pleat unpicked so the skirt remained the same length.
Can you think of a modern example?

141

Make a Pleated Top

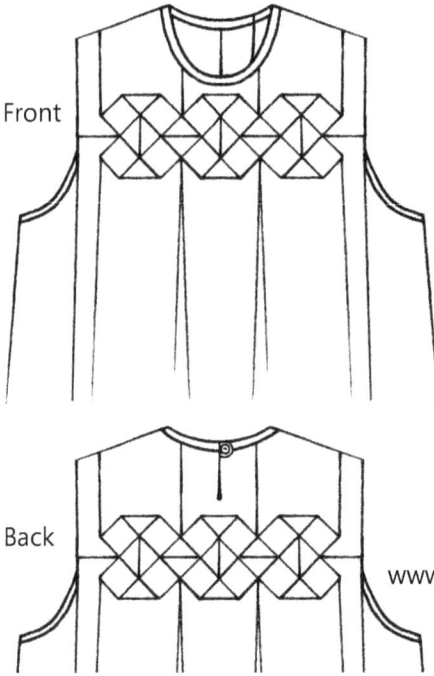

Front

Back

This top uses pleating to hold captive the fabric at the top which is released as knife pleats.

It has a bound neckline and underarms, a back neck opening, side panels and optional bust darts. It can be made any length and works well as a tunic or dress.

The pattern is minimal waste and all the pieces are rectangular, and can easily be moved around the fabric for the best layout.

A YouTube sew-a-long is here:
www.youtube.com/watch?v=1lBFzwNQTic

R/S = right side W/S = wrong side

This mindblowing pleating technique was devised by the origami artist Chris K Palmer and is detailed in the book *Shadowfolds* by Jeffrey Rutzky and Chris K Palmer. It's very effective in stripes. If you've ever done Canadian smockwork, the concept is similar - dots are marked on the wrong side, joined with thread then pulled tight to create a 3D effect on the right side. In this case the pleats lie flat rather than 3D.

You need:

✂ Woven cotton or linen fabrics which hold a crease, in plains or stripes.

✂ 1.2cm/½" bias binding for the neck and underarms (self-fabric or purchased).

✂ A button for the back neck.

✂ Two strips of fusible interfacing, 2.5cm/1" wide and the length of the neck template in your size.

✂ Perfectly matching sewing thread.

142

Pieces required

✂ Two rectangles for the **pleated panels**. One will be the back and the other the front. The length (A) and width (B) are found on the table, page 144.

For striped fabric, centre a stripe.

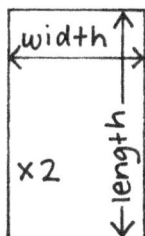

✂ Four **side panels**, cut as two pairs. The length (C) and width (D) are on the table, page 144.

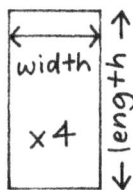

+template Use the underarm template (found on page 151) to draw in the curved top of the panel.

To cut

Cut the side panels top-and-tailed with each other like this. →
It's **very important** to make sure you have *2 pairs*, not 4 the same. The eye-shape in between the panels is not used.

The pattern pieces are designed to be modular, so you can move them around the fabric to fit.

Almost certainly your layout will look something like this:
To work out a **fabric estimate**, plug in the measurements from the table on the next page.

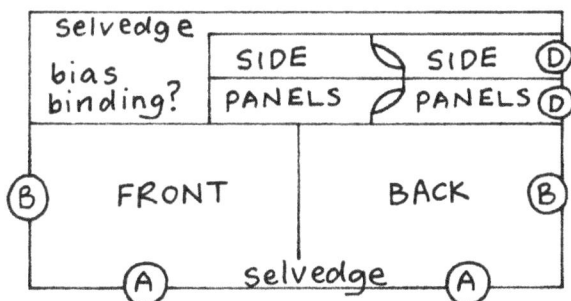

You'll have some spare fabric in handy rectangular shapes; this space could be used to cut matching bias strips for binding.

If you're cutting the garment to fit a length of fabric you already have, cut the front and back first, adding an equal amount of length on each. Then cut the side panels, adding the same amount of length.

Pick a size according to your bust measurement. The top's finished length is 13cm/5"-15cm/6" less than length (A).

Your bust measurement	86.3cm 34"	91.4cm 36"	96.5cm 38"	101.6cm 40"	106.6cm 42"	111.7cm 44"	116.8cm 46"	121.9cm 48"	127cm 50"
A Cut length of rectangle	82.2cm 32-3/8"	83.8cm 33"	85.4cm 33-5/8"	86.9cm 34-1/4"	88.5cm 34-7/8"	90.1cm 35-1/2"	91.7cm 36-1/8"	93.3cm 36-3/4"	94.9cm 37-3/8"
B Cut width of rectangle	68.5cm 27"	69.8cm 27-1/2"	71.1cm 28"	72.3cm 28-1/2"	73.6cm 29"	74.9cm/29-1/2" for all sizes onwards			
C Cut length of side panel	55.5cm 21-7/8"	57.7cm 22-3/4"	60cm 23-5/8"	62.2cm 24-1/2"	64.4cm 25-3/8"	66.6cm 26-1/4"	68.2cm 26-7/8"	69.8cm 27-1/2"	71.4cm 28-1/8"
D Cut width of side panel	11.4cm 4-1/2"	12cm 4-3/4"	12.7cm 5"	13.3cm 5-1/4"	13.9cm 5-1/2"	14.6cm 5-3/4"	15.8cm 6-1/4"	17.1cm 6-3/4"	18.4cm 7-1/4"
E Row of dots from raw edge	10.7cm 4-1/4"	11.1cm 4-3/8"	11.4cm 4-1/2"	11.7cm 4-5/8"	12cm 4-3/4"	12.3cm 4-7/8"	12.7cm 5"	13cm 5-1/8"	13.3cm 5-1/4"

Your bust measurement	132cm 52"	137.1cm 54"	142.2cm 56"	147.3cm 58"	152.4cm 60"	157.4cm 62"	162.5cm 64"	167.6cm 66"	172.7cm 68"	177.8cm 70"
A Cut length of rectangle	96.5cm 38"	98.1cm 38-5/8"	99.6cm 39-1/4"	101.2 39-7/8"	102.8cm 40-1/2"	104.4cm 41-1/8"	106cm 41-3/4"	107.6cm 42-3/8"	109.2cm 43"	110.8cm 43-5/8"
C Cut length of side panel	73cm 28-3/4"	74.6cm 29-3/8"	76.2cm 30"	77.7cm 30-5/8"	79.3cm 31-1/4"	80.9cm 31-7/8"	82.5cm 32-1/2"	84.1cm 33-1/8"	85.7cm 33-3/4"	87.3cm 34-3/8"
D Cut width of side panel	19.6cm 7-3/4"	20.9cm 8-1/4"	22.2cm 8-3/4"	23.4cm 9-1/4"	24.7cm 9-3/4"	26cm 10-1/4"	27.3cm 10-3/4"	28.5cm 11-1/4"	29.8cm 11-3/4"	31.1cm 12-1/4"
E Row of dots from raw edge	13.6cm 5-3/8"	13.9cm 5-1/2"	14.2cm 5-5/8"	14.6cm 5-3/4"	14.9cm 5-7/8"	15.2cm 6"	15.5cm 6-1/8"	15.8cm 6-1/4"	16.1cm 6-3/8"	16.5cm 6-1/2"

Make a pleating template

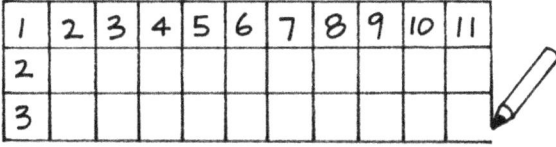

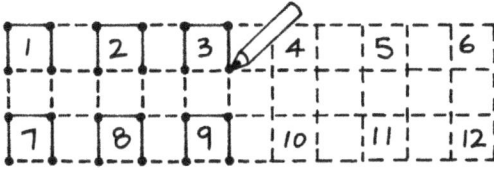

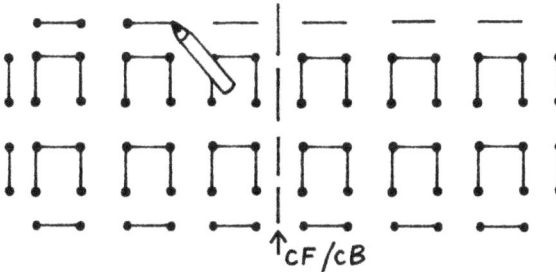

1. On paper, draw a very accurate grid of 5cm/2" squares, 11 wide by 3 high.

2. Draw in the 12 pleat positions indicated by the solid lines (upside down U shapes).

3. Surround the grid with a 4cm/1½" wide border and connect pairs of dots as shown.

At each dot, use an awl to make a hole to fit a pencil point.

Pleating the 2 panels

1. Mark the fabric's centre with a crease or line of basting. Lay the template on the *wrong* side of the fabric. Measurement (E) on the table is how far the *top line of dots* should be from the top of the fabric. Mark in the dots.

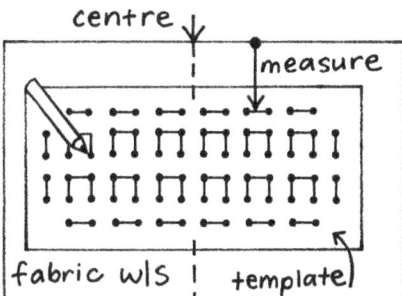

2. Thread a needle with two strands of matching thread, end unknotted. Make a *tiny* stitch at each dot, connecting them as per the template. Leave 5cm/2" tails.

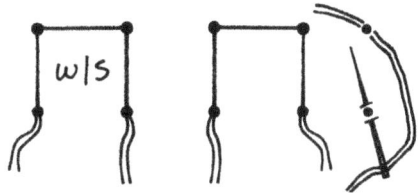

3. Pull up each pair of threads tightly and tie them together in a knot.

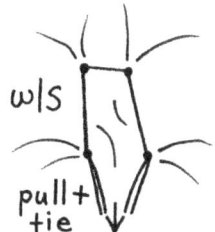

4. At the ironing board, lay it right side up and use your fingers to pull the pleating into place. Begin with the top middle pair of squares and sit them so the knife pleats point to the sides. Work out from there, following the way the knife pleats want to lie. When all are in place, press the knife pleats first (*measure so they're consistent in width*), then the squares, making sure their points touch. Below, let the pleats fall unpressed.

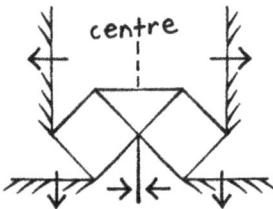

5. Cut the pleating threads to 1.2cm/½". To secure the pleats so they stay in place during laundering, flip the sections of pleating *which have vertical knife pleats* sideways and machine stitch just next to the crease (6 to do).

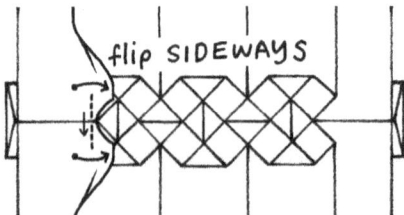

You'll only need to stitch through the part that has multiple layers of fabric, not where it's a single layer.

6. Flip the top *down* and the bottom *up*, and stitch next to the crease in the same way.

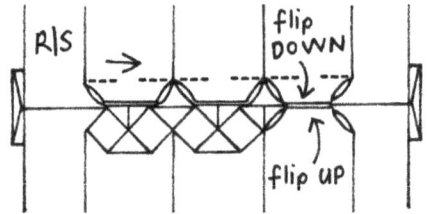

7. Finally, flip the sections *without knife pleats* sideways and stitch next to the crease (6 to do).

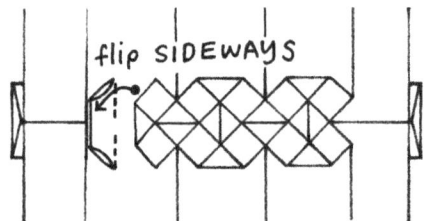

Handsew the 6 junctions together. Use a double strand of perfectly matching thread to catch the points to each other.

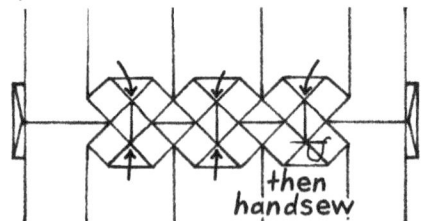

Give the pleating a good, careful press.

Decide which panel looks the best and use that for the front.

To sew

1. Cut out the back and front neckline using the neck template.

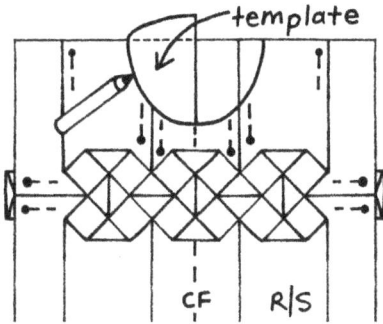

2. Stay-stitch around the neckline, shoulders and sides to hold the pleats in place.

3. On each side, measure 4cm/ 1½" down from the top for the shoulder seam.

Also, measure down from the top for the side panel placement:

Sizes 34"-36"-38": 16.5cm/6½" - 15.8cm/6¼" - 15.2cm/6"

Sizes 40"-42"-44"+: 14.6cm/5¾" - 13.9cm/5½" - 13.3cm/5¼"

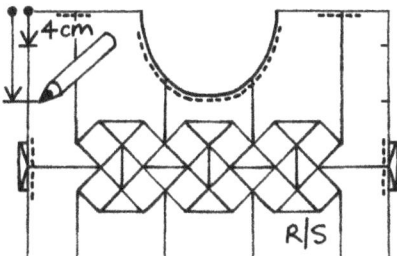

Mark these with a tiny snip or pencil mark.

4. Back neck slit. Cut the *front* neckline cutout apart like this:

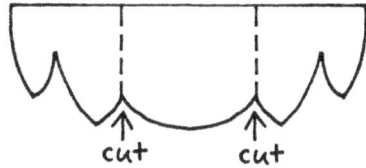

(The back neck cutout isn't used.)

5. Sew the two side pieces together as shown, taking a **6mm/ ¼" seam allowance**.

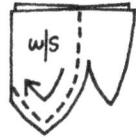

6. Turn through and press, untrimmed.

(Measure the unstitched vertical edge - in Step 8, you'll cut the slit 6mm/¼" shorter than this).

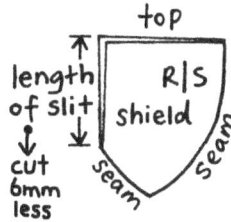

7. On the centre piece, iron on a strip of fusing 2.5cm/1" wide to the centre.

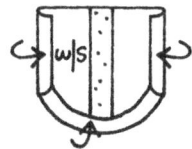

Press under the sides and bottom 6mm/¼".

On the back, iron a matching strip of fusing for the back neck slit.

147

8. Cut the slit in this piece and the back. Lay them right sides together, sandwiching the shield between them on one side.

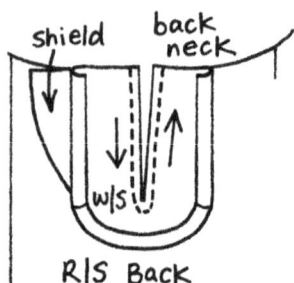

Stitch around, taking a 4mm seam, pivoting at the *bottom of the shield*.

9. Snip to the stitching's apex, turn to the inside and handsew down.

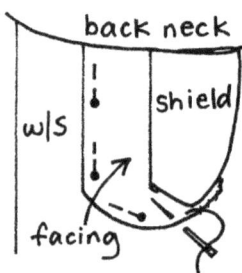

It should look like this on the right side:

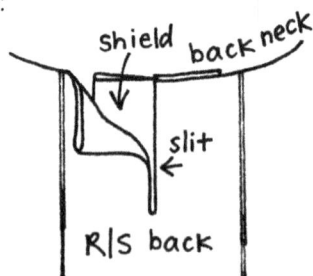

The bottom of the shield should fit snugly at the bottom of the slit, with no gap.

10. Sew the shoulder seams, taking a **1cm/⅜" seam allowance at the neck edge**, stitching to the **notch** at the side (rule a chalk line to help stitch straight)

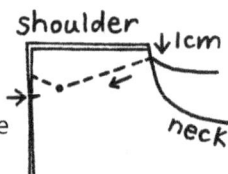

BUT 2.5cm/1" before the notch, angle the stitching *up* by 1.2cm/½". This is so you can turn back the 2.5cm/1" hem around the top armhole. Press the shoulder seams open and overlock.

✂ If you have particularly square or sloping shoulders, you can try this on pinned first, to check if the angle is right for you. Adjust if required.

11. Bind the neck, forming a button loop with one end of the binding.

Sew the button on the back.

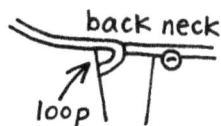

✂ If you don't have enough binding to create a loop, or if you forget to do it (or if you put it on the wrong side!), don't worry - finish each side flush and sew a press stud on instead.

148

12. On the side panels, **overlock** the short top edge and the side seam.
Stay-stitch the curved underarm.

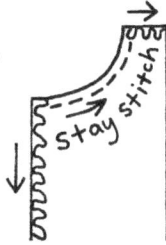
stay stitch

13. Sew the side panels to the centre panels. Match the top of the side panel to the notch and take a **6mm/¼" seam allowance**. Overlock the seams all the way over the shoulders. Press.

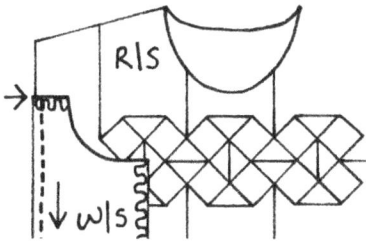
R|S
w|s

14. Press the top of the armhole 2.5cm/1" under, stopping at the horizontal knife pleats. This forms a pleat in line with the shoulder, falling unpressed.

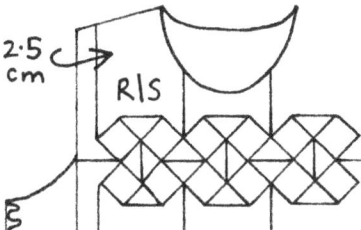
2·5 cm
R|S

15. Pin the side seams together with a 2.5cm/1" seam. Try the top

on and check the **underarm curve**. The underarm curve is deliberately high and conservative so you can fine-tune the fit on yourself.

Add **bust darts** if required. These should be in the side panel only and as horizontal as possible.

Stop the dart about 2cm/¾" short of the front panel seam. Before sewing the dart,

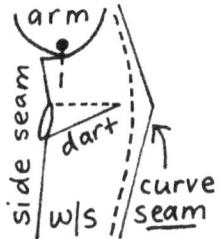
arm
side seam
dart
w|s
curve seam

unpick the front panel seam several inches above and below the dart apex. After sewing the dart, re-sew this seam and curve the edge with the dart.

When you're satisfied with the armhole, **bind** the curved edge. Ensure that the top of the binding will be well-hidden behind the armhole pleat.

16. Sew the side seam, stitching through the binding. Press open and secure at the top.

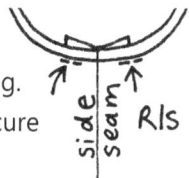
arm
side seam
R|s

17. Handsew the armhole hem and secure the top of the side panel so it's out of sight.
Hem the top to suit.

149

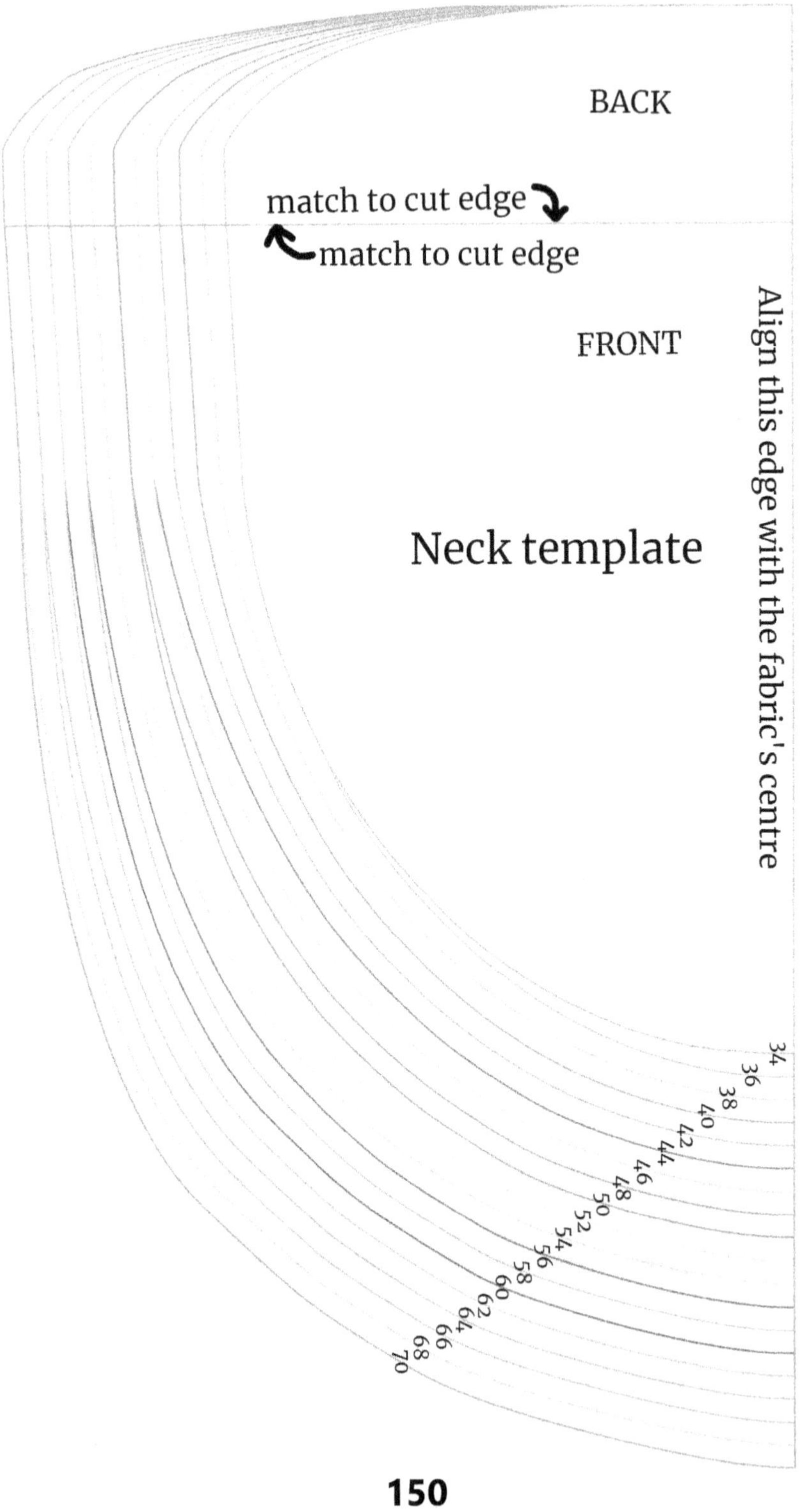
BACK
match to cut edge
match to cut edge
FRONT
Neck template
Align this edge with the fabric's centre
34
36
38
40
42
44
46
48
50
52
54
56
58
60
62
64
66
68
70

Size 44" +
Size 42"
Size 40"
Size 38"
Size 36"
Size 34"

Align with side and top of panel

Underarm template

34

36

38

40

42

44

46

48

50

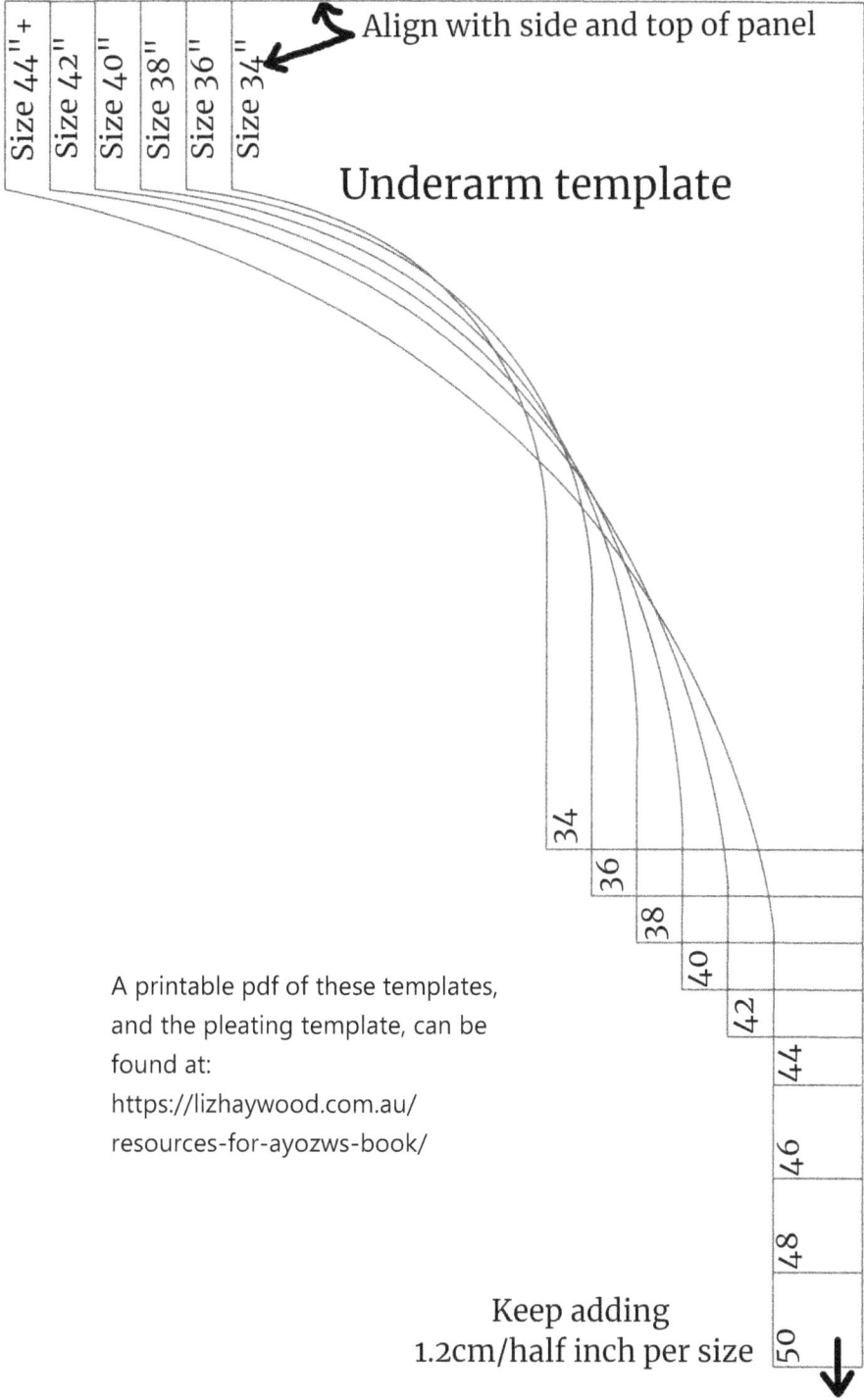

A printable pdf of these templates, and the pleating template, can be found at:
https://lizhaywood.com.au/resources-for-ayozws-book/

Keep adding
1.2cm/half inch per size

151

Zero Waste Stories

Gregory Joseph is a demi-couture made-to-measure company based in New York City, specializing in zero or near-zero waste cutting methods. They use primarily overstocked or dead stock textiles to create their collections, and being a made-to-order brand allows them to keep excess inventories at a minimum. Designer **Gregory Lagola** believes firmly in building-in longevity into each garment, and _Timelessness over Trend_ has been a company mantra from the beginning.

"I originally studied Architecture at University but after realizing that model building was not a strong suit, I switched to Physics (something about the prospect of a good paying job after graduation). At about this time, I came across an issue of W magazine, which at that time was just a small rag paper, but the cover was always graced with a beautiful fashion illustration. I was mesmerized, and couldn't stop thinking about it. It was then I started to consider the possibility of post graduate work, switched my major to Art, and graduated from Penn State University with a BA. Afterwards I made my way to New York City and studied fashion at FIT in the one-year program. From there I embarked on a long and varied career journey learning all I could from many mentors along the way.

I have always been interested in the concept of zero waste, but I never really called it that from the beginning. For me, who originally wanted to be an architect, I saw it as a challenge of wrapping an essentially two dimensional material around a

152

three dimensional body. From there I realized that even the "negative" space surrounding a cut garment could, and should, be important, so I began to consider the fabric as a massive rectilinear form that needed to be manipulated to accommodate the curves on the body. Historically of course, this has been going on for millennia, the Roman toga, the Greek chiton just to name a few. But, in my case, I wanted to explore other techniques as well and this is what keeps me motivated to move forward with this design endeavor.

There are of course challenges. As it turns out, creating zero waste garments is deceptively difficult at times. The cutting and sewing techniques required leave no room for error, and there is a certain amount of measured skill that a sewer needs to make sure all is coming together accurately. I have also found that the number of people who find zero waste compelling from a consumer point of view is rather small at the moment, but I think that number grows every year.

For me however, I find the challenge of coming up with solutions (fashion is problem solving from my point of view), to be exhilarating. I normally form the concept in my head first (many sleepless nights), and then work out the ideas in rough form in Procreate – the best application I feel for design. After that, I start working on a rough muslin, and then take the concept to one of my brilliant cutters (engineers) to work out exactly how the garment can come together. It's extremely gratifying when it works! There are things that don't come to fruition, but in most cases it's due to a lack of overall skill or prohibitive costs associated with a lot of hand work.

In the end, I am convinced that this design direction is only going to grow, There are probably thousands of solutions to zero waste cutting out there waiting to be discovered, and I'm just excited to play a small part in the effort to reduce waste and create garments of lasting beauty."

www.gregoryjoseph.com @gregoryjosephcollection

Ask Lizzy

Q: Have there been any positive surprises about designing zero waste garments?

A: Yes, lots! I didn't expect such significant fabric savings, more than could ever be achieved with conventional patternmaking. As well, I didn't fully appreciate the benefits of minimal waste. There were things I didn't think could be made zero waste and yet people tried them successfully. I hadn't realised how useful zero waste patterncutting could be to handweavers, but of course zero waste has its roots in weaving. The most positive surprise has been the friendliness of the zero waste community, in an industry that has a reputation for secrets and competitiveness.

Q: How can zero waste be more widely adopted in the fashion industry? What are some of the barriers/opportunities?

A: Zero waste patterncutting has some great opportunities for fabric economy, waste reduction and as a design tool. However, there are some high, but not impossible, barriers.

1. It's hard to shift systems to zero waste, because it's like "backwards designing". The current model of designing & making is linear with separate jobs that flow in a certain order and don't overlap: designer→ patternmaker→samplemaker→grading→cutting layout→cutting→sewing. With zero waste, the design emerges from patternmaking and sewing.

2. There aren't enough people familiar with zero waste design and patternmaking to feasibly make companies go with it. However, education is where this can change.

3. Technology is another barrier. Zero waste patterns don't fit the software systems that companies are already using. Current patternmaking/grading/ layplan software is not designed for zero waste, and the technology doesn't really exist - yet. I predict that technology will be the game-changer.

Bibilography

Buttons

✂ Thread shirt button tutorial: fabricnfiction.com/2018/01/31/tutorial-thread-shirt-buttons/

✂ Button making videos (various) by Gina-B Silkworks on YouTube.

✂ Wooden buttons tutorial: www.twigandtale.com/blogs/twig-and-tale-blog/handmade-wooden-buttons

✂ Medieval cloth stuffed buttons demonstrated by Kacy Burchfield www.youtube.com/watch?v=qUMtO0wqCqY&t=292s (10:10mins)

Eura dress and other historical reconstructions

✂ www.vikinganswerlady.com/clothing.shtml

✂ https://nattmal.wordpress.com/2018/09/04/eura-kirtle/

✂ https://medievalexcellence.com/2020/11/07/cut-and-construction-of-the-finnish-eura-underdress/

✂ https://lightwood.lochac.sca.org/garb/

Tessellations

✂ *Designing Tessellations* by J Beyer (Contemporary Books 1999)

Gussets, gores and godets

✂ http://www.renaissancetailor.com/demos_goresgussets.htm

✂ https://www.mdhistory.org/inside-mr-darcys-drawers/

Bias cut

✂ *Bias Cut Blueprints* by J Bramson and S Lenahan (Fashion in Harmony 2014)

✂ *Halston - An American Original* by E Gross and R Rottman (HarperCollins 1999)

Pleating

✂ *Complete Pleats* by P Jackson (Laurence King 2015)

✂ *Shadowfolds* by J Rutzky and CK Palmer (Kodansha 2011)

Essential Reads
(in addition to the great books in the Bibliography)

Zero Waste Cutting and Sewing
Zero Waste Fashion Design by T Rissanen and H McQuillan (Bloomsbury 2016, 2023). Strategies and techniques for zero waste patterncutting.

Zero Waste Sewing by EM Haywood (Cooatalaa Press 2020). 16 zero waste projects to make and wear, with patternmaking discussion.

Zero Waste Nähen by S Kroth (Stiebner 2022) (in German). 25 zero waste projects to wear; interesting styles and creative, innovative patternmaking.

Zero Waste Patterns by B Helmersson (Quadrille 2023). 20 projects to sew your own wardrobe, with a cool Scandi minimalist vibe.

Historical
Cut My Cote by DK Burnham (Royal Ontario Museum 1973, 1997). A slim book showing traditional clothes cut to fit the available fabric width.

The Medieval Tailor's Assistant by S Thursfield (The Crowood Press (2001). Garment cutting and sewing using archaeological and historical sources.

Medieval Garments Reconstructed (Aarhus University Press 2001). Garments found at archeology sites in Greenland, with patterns.

Costume Close-Up by L Baumgarten and J Watson (The Colonial Williamsburg Foundation 1999). 18th century garments in the collection of the Colonial Williamsburg Foundation, with patterns and construction.

Clothes From The Hands That Weave by AL Mayer (Echo Point Books 1984). Ancient woven clothing styles and construction with creative ideas for weaving and sewing them now.

Other Books

Madeleine Vionnet by B Kirke (Chronicle Books 1998). Part biography, part study of Vionnet's innovative cutting and construction.

Vionnet (Bunka Fashion College 2002) (in Japanese). 28 of Vionnet's patterns with scale layouts and sewing instructions.

Make Your Own Japanese Clothes by J Marshall (Kodansha 1988). A creative sourcebook for cutting and sewing Japanese clothes.

How to Sew Sustainably by W Ward (CICO Books 2021). 20 textile projects that reuse, refashion or are minimal waste.

Cuts of Cloth by AS Wiseman (Little, Brown & Company 1978). Traditional and modern clothing patterns, simple enough for children to make.

Creating with Shapes by U Doshi (COS 2017). Patternmaking with simple geometric shapes to produce highly original shapes and silhouettes.

Creative Dressing by K O'Connor (Routledge & Kegan Paul 1980). Cutting and sewing instructions for classic late 1970s ethnic-inspired fashion.

Vintage Menswear by Sims, Luckett and Gunn (Laurence King 2012). A collection of garment details taken from 20th century menswear.

The Art of Manipulating Fabric by C Wolff (Krause 1996). An encyclopedia of techniques that resurface, reshape, restructure and reconstruct fabric.

Modern Mending by Erin Lewis-Fitzgerald (Affirm Press 2020). The one mending book you should own.

The Dressmaker's Companion by EM Haywood (Cooatalaa Press 2017). A comprehensive sewing reference with step-by-steps, troubleshooting and fitting advice.

Acknowledgements

Much love and thanks to my dear family, who by now know that Mum's book is Zero *Waste* not *Waist*. This "Year of..." book has been with us for two years! Thank you for helping me in so many ways; I can't even begin to say how much I appreciate it. Special thanks to Lillian for editing all the sew-a-long videos.

My heartfelt thanks go to editors Anthea Martin and Nan Berrett, who guided me so much with honest opinions and advice.
Thank you so much to Stu Nankivell for another gorgeous cover, and being so easy-going to work with.
A big thank you to friends Jane Milburn, Tom Freebairn, Emily Handler, Tracy Henwood and the staff at Clare Library for your enthusiastic and unreserved help and ideas.

I sincerely thank the designers spotlighted in this book for sharing their zero waste stories and advice, and for being an inspiration to me and others: Zero Waste Design Collective, Liz Elliot, Birgitta Helmersson, Emily Klug, Ronan Silve, Emma La Rocca, Maureen Gleason, Danielle Elsener, Victoria Konash, Stefanie Kroth, Cris Wood and Gregory Lagola, and Maria Giailoglou in the zine edition.

Many thanks to the test fitting models Ann Letcher, Nigelle-ann Blaser, Lisa Koo, Jennie Cornwell, Val Freebairn and Claire Freebairn. All so giving of your time and such great sports!

Index

About the Author

Liz Haywood is a former industry patternmaker who enjoys home sewing and making things. She worked for 20 years in Australia and the UK, across a wide range of garment types, including uniforms, bridal, active wear, swimwear, made-to-measure and seasonal ranges. She also taught sewing.

For some years, Liz worked as a clothing cutter and witnessed (and helped create) the volume of fabric scraps generated by factories, which was so normal no-one even discussed it, except to ask if it was bin day.

In 2016, Liz read *Zero Waste Fashion Design* (Rissanen/McQuillan, 2016 Bloomsbury) and immediately clicked with zero waste patterncutting.

Four years later, she went hard core and decided to *only* make zero waste patterns from now on, and continues to explore the exciting challenges it brings.

Previous books by Liz Haywood are
The Dressmaker's Companion - A practical guide to sewing clothes (2017)
Zero Waste Sewing - 16 projects to make, wear and enjoy (2020)

Visit Liz's blog *The Craft of Clothes* at lizhaywood.com.au for weekly posts on sewing, fashion and zero waste patterncutting.

Resources and video links to accompany this book can be found at:
lizhaywood.com.au/resources-for-ayozws-book/

www.ingramcontent.com/pod-product-compliance
Lightning Source LLC
Chambersburg PA
CBHW032145020426
42334CB00016B/1229